REGIONAL MOBILITY AND RESOURCE DEVELOPMENT IN WEST AFRICA

Centre for Developing-Area Studies
McGill University
KEITH CALLARD LECTURES

Centre for Developing-Area Studies
McGill University
Keith Callard Lectures

REGIONAL MOBILITY AND RESOURCE DEVELOPMENT IN WEST AFRICA

by
AKIN L. MABOGUNJE

Montreal and London
PUBLISHED FOR THE CENTRE BY
McGILL—QUEEN'S UNIVERSITY PRESS
1972

© McGill–Queen's University Press 1972
Printed in Canada
by John Deyell Limited
International Standard Book Number 0–7735–0120–7 (Cloth)
International Standard Book Number 0–7735–0129–0 (Paper)
Library of Congress Catalog Card Number 79–173461
Legal Deposit 1st quarter 1972

This work has been published with the help of a grant from the Social Science Research Council of Canada using funds provided by the Canada Council.

FOREWORD

For centuries, millions of West Africans have left their homes and ethnic groups to earn their living in other countries of the region. What is most remarkable about these migrants has been their impact on West African innovation — through the introduction of new crops, the diffusion of new techniques and institutions, and the spread of new values, attitudes, and behaviour patterns.

Recognizing this vital contribution, the host societies have evolved a variety of rules and customs for receiving and accommodating these migrant peoples. But the process of accommodation has been severely disrupted in recent years. The emergence of independent nation-states has brought a wave of legislation against migrants, followed by large-scale repatriation to their lands of origin. Dr. Akin L. Mabogunje's lectures — the sixth Keith Callard series sponsored by the McGill Centre for Developing-Area Studies — take on special importance in this present-day context.

The author discusses the social and economic aspects of regional mobility in West Africa, its evolution before and during the colonial era, and its significance in the modern period of national independence. The implications of his argument would seem to be twofold: that the goals of economic development and national integration can best be achieved by strengthening the competitive position of the host peoples vis-à-vis the migrants, and not by applying repressive policies which generate further social antagonism; and that regional mobility, as opposed to development programmes imported from abroad, represents a uniquely West African approach to the area's social, economic, and political problems.

Dr. Mabogunje is currently a professor of geography at the University of Ibadan. He is also a past president of the Nigerian Geographical Association; and he has published a number of scholarly works, notably *Yoruba Towns* (1962) and *Urbanization in Nigeria* (1968). At the time of his McGill visit, in March and April 1969, he was serving as dean of the Faculty of Social Sciences at the University of Ibadan.

From the Centre's point of view, it was a productive visit indeed. Dr. Mabogunje gave freely of his time and opened up new directions for McGill research and teaching on West African development. We are very pleased to sponsor the publication of his Callard lectures; we believe them to be a major addition to the literature in this field.

IRVING BRECHER

Director
Centre for Developing-Area Studies

PREFACE

WHEN THE INVITATION to give the sixth in the series of Keith Callard Lectures came to me, I was very conscious of the fact that I was the first person from the African part of the developing world to be so honoured. In consequence, I was anxious to choose a topic which, apart from any intrinsic academic merits which it may have, reflects issues of a practical and current nature. The role of migrants in West Africa and the changing attitude to the migrants was one such topic that came to my mind. Its relevance and importance were made more pressing by the events in different parts of West Africa, especially in Nigeria, during the last few years.

In tackling the topic, I took cognizance of one of the aims of the Centre for Developing-Area Studies. This is to break down those barriers of over-specialization which prevent a rounded social-science approach to the "development" problem. I have, therefore, tried as much as is possible within the compass of four lectures to espouse a number of ideas which should generate research interest in many different fields in the social sciences. My basic concern is to call attention to the need for a different type of orientation in research endeavours into the processes of development in underdeveloped countries. This orientation emphasizes the study of those *endogenous* factors and institutions which people in developing countries have themselves used and are using in their attempts to develop. Research along these lines, to my mind, represents a vital first step towards answering the question of how to activate a society into making more determined developmental efforts.

This book is therefore aimed at those social scientists interested in exploring the problems of development in West Africa from the grass roots. In the main, the book reproduces the substance of the four lectures I gave at McGill University in March and April, 1969. I have, however, felt the need to include an introduction in order both to clear away some misconceptions and to make it easy to follow my line of arguments in the lectures.

In preparing these lectures for publication, I have had the benefit of the opinions of two of my colleagues, Professor K. M. Barbour of the Department of Geography, University of Ibadan, and Dr. Archibald Callaway of the Nigerian Institute of Social and Economic Research. Both of them may recognize sections of the book which have been improved or considerably altered as a result of their comments or criticisms. To both I wish to express my gratitude, whilst relieving them of responsibilities for any errors or contentious opinions expressed in this work.

I wish also to acknowledge the permission given me by authors and editors of journals to reproduce the following figures: figure 1 from R. Mansell Prothero, "A Typology of African Mobility," Seminar Paper, Department of Geography, University of Liverpool; figures 4 and 5 from W. B. Morgan and J. C. Pugh, *West Africa* (London: Methuen); figure 6 from Prothero, "Migrant Labour in West Africa," (Editor, *Journal of Local Administration Overseas*); figure 7 from Jean Rouch, "Les Sorkawa, pêcheurs itinérants du moyen Niger," (Editor, *Africa*); figures 8 and 10 from John M. Hunter, "Cocoa Migration and Patterns of Land Ownership in the Densu Valley near Suhum, Ghana," (Editor, *Transactions of the Institute of British Geographers);* figure 9 from Georges Savonnet, "La colonisation du pays Koulango (Haute Côte d'Ivoire) par les Lobi de Haute-Volta," (Editor, *Les Cahiers d'Outre Mer*); figure 11 from William O. Jones, *Manioc in Africa* (Stanford University Press, Food Research Institute); and figure 12 from Marguerite Dupire, "Planteurs autochtones et étrangers en Basse-Côte d'Ivoire Orientale," (Editor, *Etudes Eburnéennes*).

My greatest debt of gratitude is to Professor Irving Brecher, Director of the Centre for Developing-Area Studies, who formally invited me to McGill University to deliver the lectures; and to Professor Theo Hills, Associate Director of the Centre for Developing-Area Studies, who actually suggested my name and made all the arrangements for my visit. I wish also to register my sincere appreciation to the staff of the Centre for their help in the typing of the lectures and in making all the facilities of the Centre easily available to me. My only regret is that owing to the exigencies of my other duties at the University of Ibadan, I could not take full advantage of an anticipated three-month visit and had to be content with a three-week stay.

I would like also to thank sincerely Professor Peter Gutkind and his family who invited me to stay with them during my visit and who overwhelmed me with the warmth and generosity of their hospitality.

Finally, I acknowledge my gratitude to all those friends at McGill University who made my stay and therefore the delivering of these lectures a most exciting and pleasant experience.

CONTENTS

FIGURES

INTRODUCTION

EVERY YEAR millions of West Africans leave their homes
and kinsmen in search of profitable economic opportunities elsewhere. For many of these, the journey is a short
one. Sometimes it takes them no further than the nearest
town; sometimes it may involve a relatively longer journey to the metropolitan centre of their area; and yet at
other times, it is to wealthier rural areas, particularly
those producing agricultural raw materials for export.
As long as these journeys take place within the area occupied by their ethnic group, no serious problems of ad-
justment and reorientation arise. But for a substantial
number of West Africans, the search for fortune or extra
income takes them to the lands of other ethnic groups or
into a completely different country. It is with this latter
group that I am concerned in this study. And it is the fact
that these journeys cross ethnic or national boundaries
that has made the phrase "regional mobility" more appropriate for my purpose.

Why, it may be asked, does the subject merit detailed
examination? One can give at least several answers to
this question. In the first place, there is the sheer number
of people involved. It is estimated that in most years
probably between two and three million people move
out of their ethnic areas into the lands of other peoples
or other countries. In the second place, apart from the
short period of forced labour by the French colonial administration, much of this movement is done spontan-
eously. Unlike the situation in southern Africa, there

1

are no labour contracting firms, no specially laid on transportation arrangements, and no formalized system of advertising the economic advantages of moving. The nature of information flow, although apparently effective, remains obscure and intricate. The pattern and direction of movements are only dimly recognized. The problems of reception, housing, employment, and general social acceptance at the destination of their journeys have only started to be studied. The contribution of these migrants to the social and economic life in their new land of sojourn has just begun to be seriously evaluated.

If only for these two reasons, the subject of regional mobility compels attention by scholars. The new interpretation being given to the role and position of migrants in various West African countries makes the subject at this time even more important. Many of these countries, after the first flush of excitement over their political independence, are now faced with the sobering realities of unfulfillable but steadily rising economic expectations among their people. Migrants from other areas or countries who seem to be moderately successful become scapegoats on which to blame the economic ills of the area or country. A new mercantilist-type philosophy which sees the gains of the migrants as the loss of the indigenes or nationals is becoming widely accepted at even the highest levels of society.

Yet, because these migrants originate from all over West Africa, discriminatory policies against them in one area or country simply provoke retaliatory measures elsewhere. Especially in the last ten years, therefore, the potential for intra-national and international crises latent in regional mobility has increased tremendously. In places like Nigeria, this crisis is already with us. International frictions centred on the position of migrants have been reported between Sierra Leone and Ghana, Ivory Coast and Dahomey, Ivory Coast and Nigeria, Dahomey and Niger, Ghana and Nigeria.

It is clear therefore that the issues raised by regional mobility are of vital importance for understanding present and future economic relations among West African countries. More than this, the subject is of considerable interest because of its historical antecedents. Long before Europeans ever set foot on West African soil, people had been moving across ethnic boundaries, social norms had developed with respect to the position of such strangers in different societies, and various institutions had been established to cope with their needs and problems. All this makes a fascinating study, especially in view of the tremendous changes that have taken place in the character and number of these migrants and in the conditions of their sojourn in foreign areas.

At this juncture, it is necessary to dispel some popular misconceptions which, owing to the accidents of modern history, see the African situation as the obverse of the European experience and therefore overplay the significance of the colonial period in the development of the continent. If Europe was conceived as a developed and civilized area, with its green fields and tamed cattle, its industries, its extensive trade and commerce, Africa was imagined as a primeval and primitive area, occupied by jungles and wild animals, with no industries or trade beyond the kinship circle. Nowhere in Black Africa is this simplistic picture more misleading than in West Africa. For the purpose of this book, therefore, three of these misconceptions need to be dispelled.

The first is the idea that in West Africa before the

colonial period, ethnic groups lived in aggressive isolation. The history of this area makes it clear that peaceful movements of people outside their ethnic areas had been going on at least as far back as the eighth century A.D. during the rise of the Ghana empire. Arab writers of the period emphasized the vigour of trading activities and of movement both across the desert and within the Sudan. Ibn Battuta, writing later about the Empire of Mali in the early fourteenth century, noted that "the negroes possess some admirable qualities. They are seldom unjust and have a greater abhorrence of injustice than any other people. Their sultan shows no mercy to anyone who is guilty of the least act of it. There is complete security in their country. Neither traveller nor inhabitant in it has anything to fear from robbers or men of violence."[1] The same impression of peaceful movement and trade is conveyed by the record of Leo Africanus in his travels in the sixteenth century across the northern parts of West Africa from Oualata to Bornu.[2]

By the time of the European penetration at the beginning of the nineteenth century, we find Mungo Park indicating that on the western coastal areas Sarakole traders were to be found everywhere "in the kingdoms of Kasson, Kaarta, Ludamar and the northern parts of Bambarra."[3] About the same time Hugh Clapperton, in 1825, was mentioning the presence in the town of Kaiama of a caravan consisting of "upwards of 1000 men and women, and as many beasts of burden" on their way back to Hausaland after a long trading trip to Gonja

[1] Ibn Battuta, *Travels in Asia and Africa*, 1325-1354, trans. H. A. R. Gibb (London: Routledge, 1929), p. 329.

[2] Leo Africanus, *The History and Description of Africa*, ed. Robert Brown and trans. John Pory, vol. 3; Hakluyt Society Publications, vol. 94 (London, 1896), pp. 819-34.

[3] Mungo Park, *Travels in the Interior Districts of Africa*, vol. 1 (London: John Murray, 1816), p. 62.

and Ashanti. The headman, a native of Kano, pointed out that the caravan had been detained in Gonja for twelve months on account of the war.[4] The Landers in 1832 wrote concerning the town of Kishi in Yorubaland that "a great number of emigrants from different countries reside here: there are not a few from Borgoo, Nouffie, Haussa, and Bornou, and two or three Tuaricks, from the borders of the Great Desert."[5]

Perhaps the most detailed information on the peaceful trade movement is provided by the description of the town of Salaga in northern Ghana in a report by Captain Lonsdale to the British Parliament in 1882.

> Salaga is strictly a trader's town . . . whether it became a place of importance prior to the Ashanti era, or whether the Ashantis made the market, is a question the answer to which it is difficult to drag out of the obscurity enveloping the past history of this and all other countries in this part of Africa. . . . Irrespective of the Hausas, who come for the kola nut alone, there are many who trade from their country to places such as Sansanne Mango, Safara, Hombori and Timbuktu, from which they bring to Salaga cloths of various kinds differing from those of Hausa manufacture, ivory, cattle, and sheep. Then again, some make Salaga their headquarters for from two to three years, trading backwards and forwards to places within 60 days' journey. . . . There is the Mosi with his cattle, sheep and slaves. . . . The natives of Dagomba, Sansanne Mango, and the many small countries of the interior with cattle, sheep, ivory, skins of wild animals, . . . traders from Lagos

4 Hugh Clapperton, *Journal of a Second Expedition into the Interior of Africa* (London: John Murray, 1829), p. 68.

5 Richard and John Lander, *Journal of an Expedition to Explore the Course and Termination of the Niger*, vol. 1 (London: John Murray, 1832), p. 204.

with coast produce; . . . the whole presents a very animated though exceedingly hot scene.[6]

It is possible to multiply references such as these to attest to considerable mobility and interaction among the peoples of West Africa long before the European penetration of the area. Except for occasional periods of conflict and three centuries of the transatlantic slave trade when life and property became highly insecure, these movements were free and generally unprovocative in nature. What the colonial period achieved was first, to re-create the conditions making for free movements of people, and secondly, to considerably stimulate these movements. The former it did through establishing a more permanent situation of peace and order; the latter through improvements in transportation by rail, road, sea, and air.

The second misconception is the often unspoken belief that in West Africa there is an abiding and permanent hatred or antagonism among the various ethnic groups. This belief is particularly prevalent among a class of foreign scholars whose brief contacts with African problems are made in terms of the competitive politics of the post-colonial era. This misconception tends to ignore age-long cordial inter-ethnic relations under different political arrangements, and it puts the colonial administration in the position of a benign referee holding back warring ethnic antagonists from one another's throat. Its danger is that it tries to explain the crises to which I have referred above in these rather over-simplified terms, thereby discouraging further analysis.

The final misconception to discard is what I have called "the lack of development" thesis. This misconception sees Africa as an area of the world where devel-

---

[6] See Freda Wolfson, ed., *Pageant of Ghana* (London: Oxford University Press, 1958), pp. 183-85.

opment has been nearly static since almost the end of the Neolithic period. It is, of course, true that Africa has not experienced anything as spectacular as the Industrial Revolution in Europe. It is also true that while Europe was making tremendous technological strides, Africa seemed deep in the throes of a dark age of slave trading. These factors, however, did not mean that development of a less spectacular and less pervasive type was not taking place in different parts of the continent. In fact, one of the principal agencies for these positive changes was the migrant transmitting information, techniques, and artefacts from one area to another. When more peaceful conditions returned and opportunities for innovative activities expanded, the migrant came to play again a very prominent role in resource development all over West Africa.

It is important to dispel these popular misconceptions because not only do they distort reality, but they also prevent an appreciation of historical continuity in the development of West Africa. The time perspective allows us to see many of the consequences of regional mobility as a continuous adaptation and modification of traditional norms and institutions to meet new social and economic needs. In the third chapter, I have given particular prominence to this aspect of the problem. There, in fact, I have argued that those arrangements, organizations, and institutions that have evolved to facilitate the economic activities of migrants must themselves be considered as resources. Most of these have their origin in traditional organizations, but have been adapted for the particular purpose of migrants abroad. This element of historical continuity is important, since it indicates more forcibly one way through which developmental process in West Africa can be rapidly activated. I have, therefore, called attention to the need for scholars to study these various institutions not as anthropological curios but as examples of indigenous efforts at self-improvement that may hold important clues for more organized attempts at planning for economic development.

The historical perspective has one other importance. The movements of people do not take place in a vacuum; their volume and direction are affected by the level of political organization and the pattern of political relationships at any particular period. Whilst the former often determines the extent of the area over which uninterrupted movement can take place, the latter determines the status and degree of social acceptability of the migrants. West Africa is occupied by a large number of ethnic polities, some very large but most quite small. Historically, the relation between these various ethnic-based political units has been very fluid and changeable. Large empires have arisen and after a time declined. Whilst they lasted, they facilitated trade, travels, and migrations among their constituent ethnic groups. Kingdoms have developed which, by accepting the bond of common ancestry, created the conditions of general acceptability for their various people. On the other hand, some areas remained for most of known history at the margin of the ebb and flow of these important political developments, and their people hardly participated in any long-distance movements away from home.

The colonial period stands out in West Africa because it saw the consolidation of situations that stimulated trade, travels, and migrations among different ethnic groups to an unprecedented level. Although the colonial powers imposed a new framework of political organizations, they also provided more sophisticated institutions and technologies for facilitating human movement. However, because of their essential aloofness from the myriads of ethnic groups over which they ruled, new situations were created with respect to the relations between migrants and their hosts. Over wide areas of economic activities and social relations, foreign laws and conventions were imposed which bound both the migrants and their hosts and ignored the differences between their traditional practices. As long as the colonial administration lasted, there was no strong need to examine these differences and adjust them in the light of changing circumstances. All social efforts at this time were directed first towards imbibing the culture and later towards throwing off the yoke of the colonial powers.

With independence and the intense competition for political power, the problems posed by these relations have become paramount for the new African states. They have become important for both the internal cohesion of the new states and their political relations with one another. Especially with respect to the latter, there is a need to resolve the complicated issue of the nationality of migrant people living within the area of a new state at the time of independence. For example: Is an Hausa, whose great-grandparents migrated from Northern Nigeria to the area which now constitutes the modern state of Ghana and who has lived there all his life, a Ghanaian or a Nigerian? Are place of birth and residence criteria in determining nationality or does ethnic affiliation determine for all times the nationality of a West African?

It is clear that an historical perspective provides vital insight into the problems of regional mobility in West Africa. Furthermore, it is obvious that, for the purpose of these chapters, a twofold division of the historical period into pre-national and national represents a convenient device for indicating changes in the position of

9

migrants, their relations with their host communities, and the conditions which facilitate or impede their movement and determine their economic effectiveness.

Compared to other parts of Black Africa, West Africa stands in an almost unique position. It is an area where European colonization in the form of permanent settlement never took firm roots and where, as a result, the problems examined in these chapters place very little emphasis on race relations or racial conflicts. West Africa is par excellence the land of the Blacks. It is also that part of Black Africa where man had attained a relatively high level of political and economic organization before the advent of Europeans. This is attested to by the impressive history of empires and kingdoms, by the long tradition of extensive trade and commercial relations, by the presence of large and ancient cities, and by the great economic vigour and aggressiveness of many of its peoples.

In this study, West Africa is defined as that area bounded on the north by the Sahara Desert, on the west and south by the Atlantic Ocean, and on the east by the Cameroon-Adamawa Highland. It has an area of 2.4 million square miles and, in 1964, it had a population of 94 million, 99.95 per cent of whom are of African descent. In recent times, this area has been divided into fifteen political units. Thirteen have a population of less than 5 million each; one, that is, Ghana, has a population of nearly 8 million and another, Nigeria, has a population of over 50 million. This pattern of population distribution, since it determines the relative importance of migrants in any population, will be shown to have great significance for the present attitude of many West African states to the question of regional mobility.

In this introduction, I have set the stage for the discussions to follow. I have emphasized why regional mobility is becoming an increasingly important issue in West Africa and have pointed out that the extensive movements of people are not a new phenomenon in West Africa. In order to underline the need to keep an historical perspective on the matter, I have tried to dispel some popular misconceptions. This study, however, is concerned with regional mobility and resource development. The fundamental questions which are posed are therefore in terms of the relation between these two topics. What is the role of migrants in development? What aspects of their experience as migrants equip them pre-eminently for this role? What should be the attitude of governments in the new West African states to this class of people?

The plan of this book, however, needs a little comment. I begin by providing a theoretical framework; the first chapter explores, on a largely speculative plane, the social and psychological transformation involved in the act of migration and the effect of this on the attitude to innovation and resource development. It considers how social, economic, and technological conditions co-existing at any one period influence the effectiveness of migrants as agents of development. Attention is also given to defining what is meant here by resource development. It is emphasized that this is not necessarily the same thing as economic development.

The second chapter discusses the pattern and magnitude of regional mobility. It examines different types of mobility and, in particular, the massive labour migrations that developed with the progress of the colonial era. This type of mobility in search of short-term wage employment in farms, mines, or public works, whilst numerically impressive, is not the main concern of these chapters. Here, attention is focused on the movements

11

of free, enterprising individuals, whether farmers, traders, artisans, or missionaries, who move into an area and through their labour, ingenuity, or acumen succeed in creating new wealth for themselves. It may be that originally many of these people were wage-labour migrants and, having accumulated some capital, struck out on their own. This phenomenon would simply emphasize that the two groups are not mutually exclusive without obscuring the distinction between them. This chapter also examines the historical origins of the two groups of migrants, their social characteristics, and the changing pattern of the reception accorded them by the host country.

The third chapter explores the relation between regional mobility and resource development. It uses a number of fairly well-documented examples to stress the development and diffusion of institutions, techniques, material goods, and appropriate social values resulting from the activities of migrants. Although, unfortunately, there is a lack of quantitative data, this chapter expresses the view that a considerable amount of agricultural output, commercial transactions, and investment activity is accounted for in many West African countries by migrants.

The final chapter examines the future of regional mobility in the changing political scene in West Africa. Pan-Africanism appears everywhere to be on the retreat. It is being replaced by economic chauvinism which sees the contribution of the migrants resulting not from their special circumstances but from an usurpation of "the rights and privileges" of members of the host community. Restriction rather than competition is now the battle cry. Instead of positive programmes to strengthen the competitive effectivenesss of indigenes or nationals vis-à-vis the immigrants, most governments are too tempted by the short-term political advantage of sacrificing the interests of the immigrants on the altar of national cohesion. The chapter ends by pointing out that if the desired West African Economic Community whose Articles of Association were signed in Accra, Ghana, on 4 May 1967 is to come to fruition, then the free movement of enterprising individuals has to be generally accepted and guaranteed across the whole of West Africa.

CHAPTER I:
A THEORETICAL FRAMEWORK
FOR REGIONAL MOBILITY

REGIONAL MOBILITY is used here to cover only those movements of individuals and groups of individuals that take place across ethnic or national boundaries. Whilst this definition does not exclude the more conventional types of movements, such as the rural-urban, rural-rural, or urban-urban movements, it insists that their trajectories must cross ethnic or national boundaries. The word "mobility" has also been used in preference to "migration" because of its less restrictive connotation. The *Oxford English Dictionary* defines mobility simply as "ability to move" or "capacity to change place."[1] The *Encyclopaedia of the Social Sciences,* on the other hand, defines migration as "the movements of people over considerable distances and on a large scale with the intention of abandoning their former homes for some more or less permanent new domicile."[2] The critical idea in this definition of migration is that it relates to a change of residence. Indeed, all studies of migration concentrate on this aspect of the movement and, to a greater or lesser extent, consider what the migrants do at their new domicile. But mobility need not imply any "intention of abandoning . . . former homes." Indeed, if any intention can be deciphered, it is that of making

1 *Oxford English Dictionary,* 1933 ed., s.v. "mobility."
2 Roland B. Dixon, "Migration," *Encyclopaedia of the Social Sciences,* ed. Edwin R. A. Seligman (New York: Macmillan, 1930), p. 420. See also, P. A. Sorokin, "Mobility," ibid., p. 554.

the former home a better place to return to periodically or at the end of the foreign sojourn.

Furthermore, other ideas are implicit in the concept of mobility which are worthy of consideration. The *Encyclopaedia of the Social Sciences* defines only the social dimension of the concept. It sees social mobility as the movement of individuals or groups of individuals from one social stratum to another as well as the dissemination of cultural objects, values, and behaviour patterns amongst them. The Encyclopaedia goes further to distinguish two types of mobility: horizontal and vertical. Horizontal mobility occurs when the transition takes place through either migration of people or the shifting and diffusion of cultural objects among individuals or groups on the same social level. Vertical mobility involves the movement of individuals or groups from one social stratum to another. There are two points in this definition that call for special emphasis. The first is that, in mobility, attention is paid not only to the persons moving but also to the cultural objects, values, traits, and institutions that are being disseminated by them. This idea is seldom encountered in discussions on migrations. But it needs to be kept very much in the foreground if we are to have a proper perspective on the resource importance of population movements in West Africa. The second point relates to that aspect of horizontal mobility involving a transition which can occur through migration of people. In this respect, horizontal mobility comes very close to my conception of regional mobility. The only difference is that whilst the definition of migration ignores the existence of frontiers and boundaries, that of mobility recognizes their importance in relation to both the numbers and the social acceptability of migrants in the host country.

To show the appropriateness of this definition for the

West African situation, it remains to examine more clearly what is implied by the idea of groups on the same social level or at the same stage of socio-economic development. For instance, it has been suggested that certain indices can be used to identify different levels or stages of development. Among these are income, standard of living, prestige, occupational status, educational privileges, and duties. For West Africa, it is possible to apply each or all of these indices and get meaningful though obvious results. It seems to me, however, that there is another means of illustrating the accuracy of the definition of mobility and, in the process, of defining the conceptual framework more rigorously in terms of actual life situations. This alternative method, moreover, enables us to set up a typology of the social and economic contexts within which regional mobility can and does take place.

SOCIAL FRAMEWORK FOR REGIONAL MOBILITY

Mobility, any type of human mobility, gives rise to interaction. This occurs between the individuals or groups moving and the community or social stratum into which they are moving. The diverse processes involved in this interaction have been the concern, in particular, of that branch of the social sciences known as human ecology. Robert E. Park and Ernest W. Burgess, early proponents of this field of study, suggest that social interaction involves four chief processes: competition, conflict, accommodation, and assimilation. According to Park, "the community and the natural order within the limits of the community . . . are an effect of competition. Social control, and the mutual subordination of individual members to the community have their origin in conflict, assume definite organised forms in the process of accommodation, and are consolidated and fixed in assimilation."[3]

Although each process is relevant to a discussion of regional mobility, it is the last of the four—assimilation —that is at present of crucial importance to our conceptual exploration. Park, in a different context, suggests that social assimilation "as popularly used is a political rather than a cultural concept. It is the name given to the process or processes by which people of diverse racial origins and different cultural heritages, occupying a common territory, achieve a cultural solidarity sufficient at least to sustain a national existence."[4] Park illustrates his point in terms of the Chinese in America and the Europeans in China. These migrants accommodate themselves to the conditions of life in a foreign country by learning the native language but not by adopting, except to a very slight degree, the native customs. According to Park, one of the conditions which determine and limit the progress of assimilation is a type of "self-consciousness which in the case of the immigrant assumes the form of racial or national consciousness." The same condition of racial or national consciousness on the part of the host community can also make assimilation difficult, even for a willing migrant.

In considering the West African case, I would suggest that another equally important condition which may encourage or hinder easy assimilation is the extent to which the economy of the host community has become industrialized. These two ideas—the degree of national consciousness and the degree of industrialization—facilitate setting up a typology of the social contexts within which assimilation takes place.

However, instead of "national consciousness," I prefer

3 Robert E. Park and Ernest W. Burgess, *Introduction to the Science of Sociology* (Chicago: University of Chicago Press, 1921), p. 785.
4 Park, "Assimilation, Social," *Encyclopaedia of the Social Sciences*, p. 281.

to use the word "nationhood" for reasons which will soon become obvious. The crucial element in this word is the suffix "hood," meaning simply "state, condition or fact of being." Nationhood, therefore, means no more than the fact or condition of being declared a nation or, to be more precise, of being internationally accepted as a political state possessing the legal attributes of territoriality, sovereignty, and legitimacy.

It is quite possible to identify the stage when nationhood or the status of being a nation comes about. For many parts of Africa and Asia, this is a well-marked and dramatic phenomenon. Independence is the day when the flag of the erstwhile colonial masters is pulled down, and the flag of the new nation with its bright colours and novel symbols is unfurled. This occasion in the life of the people in the area is a conspicuous watershed. One can therefore talk of a pre-national and a national period, the former stretching virtually from pre-history to the end of the colonial regime, the latter starting with the transfer of power to the new "home-grown" political elite.

This dichotomy between pre-national and national societies provides the first basis for building a typology. The second basis is provided by industrialization, which can be defined as "the system of production that has arisen from the steady development, study, and use of scientific knowledge."[5] It involves not only the use of power-driven machines but also the organization of production on the principles of specialization and the division of labour. In consequence, its primary emphasis is to increase total productivity whilst minimizing real costs per unit of product. This emphasis on efficiency gradually comes to permeate all areas of economic life.

5 J. R. T. Hughes, "Industrialization: Economic Aspects," *International Encyclopedia of the Social Sciences*, ed. David Sills (New York: Macmillan and The Free Press, 1968), p. 252.

In the process, social relations come to be greatly influenced by achievement, universalism, and functional specificity rather than by ascription, particularism, and functional diffuseness.

It is possible to extend further this definition of industrialization. I believe, however, that the present definition provides the salient features of the economic aspects of this eighteenth-century revolution in human history. What is more important for our purpose is to delineate from this definition what a pre-industrial economic order looks like. Apart from the absence of chemical and power-driven equipment for production, the pre-industrial order is not the exact opposite of the industrial. Rather, the difference between the two orders is in terms of scale, intensity, and therefore, effectiveness of organization. Pre-industrial society was aware of the value of scientific knowledge, but it neither prosecuted its study (or use) for its own sake nor was it concerned with seeing to its steady development. If through chance or the whim of a ruler some innovative idea or technique became available, it was absorbed into the stock of cultural objects or traits. In the same way, the idea of specialization based on functional division of labour was also known, as is evidenced by the presence of specialist producers in urban centres of pre-industrial societies. But the small scale of operation and the limited range of mechanical aids available to the producers restricted their economic effectiveness. Moreover, their dependence on animate power (of man and beast) with its susceptibility to fatigue, illness, boredom, or delinquency also limited the scale and range of possible specialization.

More important are the differences between the two orders in organizational and intellectual aids to production. These differences can be most clearly illustrated in terms of the organizational framework for the supply of the four main factors of production: capital, land, labour, and entrepreneurship. In the pre-industrial order, the supply of capital to a production unit came largely from the individual proprietor or his kinsmen. Although studies in a number of developing societies today reveal also the institution of rotating credit groups, most of these are or have been based on individuals well known or closely related to one another. Even where such credit groups rose to the status of virtual lending banks, they remained a family or kinship-based organization. By contrast, the industrial order has evolved the joint-stock banking institution based on the accumulation of the relatively small savings of a large number of unrelated individuals. This allows considerable credit facilities to be extended to many other people quite unrelated to those making the savings.

The limitation of access to capital in pre-industrial societies means in effect that production units are generally small and almost invariably one-man or family businesses. The basic organization comprises the master, one or two journeymen, and a few apprentices. The joint-stock company or corporation of the industrial age with its elaborate chain of order and responsibilities, and with participants ranging from the board of directors through the managing director to the most unskilled recruit, is in sharp contrast to the cottage-size organization of business in pre-industrial societies.

The difference in the provision and training of labour is also remarkable. In the pre-industrial order the provision and training of labour is undertaken within the family. Only members of a family can learn the trades or skills for which the family is noted. The period of apprenticeship starts almost as soon as one is old enough to understand the use of words and continues until puberty. Such skills—as well as the number of families who have them—are usually few, and knowledge of them is guarded very zealously. Madeline Manoukian, for instance, pointed out that among the Akan of Ghana, the *adwumfo* or goldsmiths "were in olden days an honoured class; they formed a sort of brotherhood and were privileged to wear gold ornaments, otherwise restricted to kings and their wives, and greater chiefs. The art was retained in certain families."[6] Among the Yoruba of south-western Nigeria, Daryll Forde explains that "craft specialists, both men and women, are organised into guilds with recognised heads. Such crafts are often quasi-hereditary in certain *idile* or 'compounds,' a large proportion of the members of which practise the craft in question. In some chiefdoms all the principal guilds including women's were represented on the State Council. No one is allowed to practise any craft unless admitted as a member of the appropriate guild. . . . The guilds protect the interests of their members."[7] Indeed, in some areas the community as a whole provides sanctions to reinforce the monopoly rights of the guilds. Horace Miner gives a vivid description of the situation which he found in the pre-industrial society of the ancient city of Timbuktu in West Africa. "The craft organization of pre-French days," he writes, "was supported by supernatural sanctions, physical force, popular consensus and the right to select apprentices. . . . If anyone but an apprenticed Arma tries to sew leather slippers, it is believed that the needle will turn against him and prick his hand. If a person who is not from a family of masons tries to build a house, he will topple from the wall to his death. . . . No house owner would have his house repaired by a mason who was not from the

6 Madeline Manoukian, *The Akan and Ga-Adangme Peoples of the Gold Coast* (London: Oxford University Press, 1950), p. 21.

7 Daryll Forde, *The Yoruba-Speaking Peoples of South-Western Nigeria* (London: Oxford University Press, 1951), p. 16.

builder's family because the owner would not want his house to collapse."[8]

Certainly, modern trade unions would be more than gratified if society were to support their closed-shop policy with such fervour and metaphysical conviction. However, such a situation would be difficult to achieve in modern societies given the facts that labour recruitment in industries is no longer based on such a particularistic criterion as kinship and that training is more formal and clearly defined.

However, one must not give the impression that the pre-industrial order is static and unvariegated with respect to these arrangements. In different parts of West Africa today, one finds a continuous gradation in the apprenticeship system as well as in the method of recruiting into the system.[9] More and more, the emphasis is shifting from recruiting only kinsmen into a craft business. Today, in most workshops, one finds not only members of other local families but also people of other ethnic groups. A variety of contractual agreements now binds the master and the apprentice, defining the length of apprenticeship, the scope of training, and the obligations of the two parties. In some cases also, training is becoming more formal and organized. Furthermore, small tools and mechanical aids now complement traditional craft skills while, in some cases, modern small-scale enterprises such as photography and bicycle-repairing are organized as if they were traditional crafts.

It is perhaps in the supply of entrepreneurship and management that some of the most significant contrasts persist between pre-industrial and industrial societies.

[8] Horace Miner, *The Primitive City of Timbuctoo* (Princeton, N.J.: Princeton University Press, 1953), pp. 54-55.

[9] See, for instance, Archibald Callaway, "Nigeria's Indigenous Education: The Apprentice System," *Odu: University of Ife Journal of African Studies*, 1, no. 1 (July 1964): 62-79.

In pre-industrial societies, the role of the guilds is crucial in this respect. Various craft guilds exist not only to protect the interests of the hereditary families but also to ensure that standards and quality are maintained in the production of craft goods. For this purpose, the guilds operate almost in the capacity of a super-management. This protective role, because it minimizes the unsettling effects of competition, has been most inimical to the growth of innovative entrepreneurship. Within the guild itself such "breaking of new ground" is likely to be frowned upon with justifiable reason. Except where the changes being introduced are of an inconsequential nature, a family that suddenly discovers or invents a new technique for significantly improving the quality or quantity of production and is allowed to exploit this advantage would soon come to dominate the guild and displace many other families from the trade.

Henri Pirenne, in describing the situation of pre-industrial Europe in the Middle Ages, made the point very succinctly.

> Everywhere the fundamental traits [of the craft guild] were the same. . . . Its essential aim was to protect the artisan, not only from external competition, but also from the competition of his fellow-members. . . . It was on this account that more and more minute regulations governed a technique which was strictly the same for all. . . . The result was to safeguard the independence of each by the vigorous subordination of all. The counterpart of the privilege and monopoly enjoyed by the guild was the destruction of all initiative. No one was permitted to harm others by methods which enabled him to produce more quickly and more cheaply than they. Technical progress took on the

appearance of disloyalty. The ideal was stable conditions in a stable industry.[10]

In these circumstances, innovative entrepreneurship in pre-industrial societies was often supplied by strangers and traders. These people, because they have to move from one community to another, find themselves in a position to observe and compare the type, quality, and style of goods produced by each community and to stimulate trade in these goods. Sometimes their action may also lead to the transfer of technical know-how between the communities. Alternatively, this may happen by members of a craft family migrating to another place, where such a craft is not as yet established. Or it may result from a stranger who, in having to define an economic or social relationship with his new host, thinks out a novel way of doing things. Eventually, however, these innovations become absorbed into the formal structure of guilds, customs, or usages in the area.

It may, of course, be argued that I have overstressed the restrictive role of the guilds and overplayed the innovative activities of strangers and migrants. I am even willing to accept that not all guilds are restrictive to the same extent. Indeed, for the traders' guild, internal restrictions of what goods to vend would be a contradiction in terms. But for the craft and service guilds, such restrictions may be seen more as a factor of survival. Furthermore, I agree that in West Africa today the role of the guilds has changed considerably. Their ability to enforce restriction has been considerably weakened by the withdrawal of civic sanctions and the increasing liberalization of social life due to education. I also accept the argument that, in this situation, the problem of development of pre-industrial enterprises is not so much

10 Henri Pirenne, *Economic and Social History of Medieval Europe* (London: Kegan Paul, Trench, Trubner & Co., 1936), pp. 185-86.

the restrictive activities of the guilds as the existence of a technological ceiling to their expansion, of a relatively limited market for their products, and of a shortage of real management skills. Nor would I contend that strangers and migrants are the only agency for change in pre-industrial societies. Nonetheless, when all this has been conceded, it remains largely true that the historical role of guilds has been to resist change and development, whilst that of migrants and traders has been to stimulate them.

Finally, there is the factor of land not only in production but also in the interaction between individuals and groups. In pre-industrial societies, access to land was determined by membership of particular families. A valid distinction was made between the use—or usufruct —and the ownership of land. The right to use land resided with the individual and could even be transferred to non-family members. The ownership of land was a different matter. It resided permanently in the family as a corporate entity and could not be alienated by any of its individual members. This is not to say that under certain circumstances, the corporate family, acting in concert or through its accredited representative, could not alienate part of its land by gift or even by sale. But such events in pre-industrial societies were few and far between. Indeed, it can be shown that there was no urgent necessity for it. Given the poor transportation situation in pre-industrial societies, the extent and importance of the exchange economy was usually greatly circumscribed. The urge to produce agricultural commodities far in excess of the needs of one's family was not strong. Applied to the demand for land, this fact would also mean that most families would be satisfied with a small amount of land. And although they may stake a pre-emptive right over a much larger area, it was often to allow for growth in the size of the family or dependants. The development of an exchange economy is clearly incompatible with such a conception of the value of land. And industrialization, to the extent that it heightens the tempo of exchange in an economy, invariably throws the right of land ownership into the melting pot of negotiable assets. The problem is, of course, vastly different in a socialist economic system where land, like other factors of production, is owned by the state and exchange is organized on bases other than that of profit.

Nonetheless, these economic contrasts between pre-industrial and industrial societies do seem to have equally important social correlates. Most conspicuous and far-reaching are those of the role and significance of kinship. In many pre-industrial societies, the constellation of kinsmen constitutes the major source of social position and personal identification. The hereditary basis of these positions means that there is no likelihood of a non-kinsman aspiring to, or attaining, them. Strangers and migrants, irrespective of any contribution they may make to the life of the community, would always remain strangers and migrants, since there is no niche in the hereditary ascriptive system into which they can be fitted. At best, a parallel but separate system can be built for them in the segregated neighbourhood of the stranger's quarters—the *sabon garis* or *zongos* of West Africa. Here, they may be chiefs, even hereditary chiefs; they may become men of substance and importance; they may even become famous and renowned. But always they remain strangers, living on the sufferance of their hosts and regarded socially as having slightly inferior status.

Such social rigidities are clearly incompatible with industrialization, whether organized on a capitalist or socialist basis. Wilbert E. Moore, in his illuminating study, *The Impact of Industry*, emphasizes that industrialization, because of its insistence on extensive mobility, almost by definition, must break up the large kinship organizations of pre-industrial societies.[11] The mobility is on the one hand geographical, "involving a concomitant physical separation of kinsmen." On the other hand, it is social, involving the separation of kinsmen in their "social status and styles of life. The respective fates of adult siblings—to say nothing of cousins—may be very different in competitive economic placement."

Moore goes on to say that perhaps even more damaging to the social importance of lineage is the intergenerational mobility set up by industrialization. In industrial societies, hereditary rights become widely superseded by "status assignments based on individual qualities and achievements." Age becomes less important in defining social and economic relations. Young and capable men of proven talent can rise to the highest level in society. The inter-generational mobility which is thereby set up is essential not only " for continuous changes in occupational distributions" but also for continuing economic growth. "The demand that all kinsmen 'share and share alike' would set impossible restrictions on an industrial system based on efficient labour allocation and mobility."

The nature of mobility within an industrial system thus provides the stranger and the migrant with the opportunity to assimilate and be assimilated. Because status assignment in the system depends on his own individual qualities and achievements, he can aspire to any position. Modern industrial societies still set artificial barriers to mobility on the basis of race or creed. But these barriers cannot exist indefinitely against the

11 Wilbert E. Moore, *The Impact of Industry* (Englewood Cliffs, N.J.: Prentice-Hall, 1965), pp. 86-87.

current of forces which must eventually destroy them.

This outline of the differences in the economic and social structure of pre-industrial and industrial societies has been necessary to enable us to build up a typology of situations within which the impact and importance of regional mobility can be examined. What has been shown is that these two variables—nationhood and industrialization—can be said to have two states, a "pre-existent" and an "existent" state. Theoretically, they can both be combined to give four possible situations: a pre-national, pre-industrial situation; a pre-national, industrial situation; a national, pre-industrial situation; and a national, industrial situation.

It is necessary to emphasize that by treating conditions that are almost in constant change, as if they were dichotomous, I have done a harsh injustice to reality. My only plea would be that this is necessary for the purpose of analysis, which, as always, cannot treat reality in wholeness but in dissection. Moreover, not all of the four theoretically possible situations are necessarily identifiable in real life. For instance, it is difficult to conceive of the second situation in which an area is already industrialized but remains in a pre-national state. Industrialization, by facilitating the effectiveness of communication, tends, as Karl Deutsch rightly points out, to strengthen the awareness of common nationality.[12]

On the other hand, the pre-national, pre-industrial situation characterized most of Africa up to and including the colonial period. The colonial period, however, represented a significant transition. In a political sense, it shared the lack of national particularism of the pre-national period. But it also witnessed the laying of the

[12] Karl W. Deutsch, *Nationalism and Social Communication* (Cambridge, Mass. and New York: The Technology Press and John Wiley & Sons, 1953), p. 73.

foundation of the social and economic system of the national period. Since 1957, the continent has moved to the national, pre-industrial state and is striving towards the national, industrial situation. The fact that West African countries are in this critical phase of emerging from a pre-national status to nationhood and are gradually becoming industrialized is of crucial importance in appreciating the significance of and prospects for regional mobility in the area.

In this study, I do not allude to the industrial situations; regional mobility within this context has received considerable attention in the literature. In particular, it dominates studies of emigration from the Old World to the New World, especially to North America. Moreover, even when problems of assimilation arise in these areas due, for instance, to racial or religious differences, the nature of their resolution is of an entirely different order from that which I intend to expound in these chapters.

DEFINING RESOURCE DEVELOPMENT

Here again, in my analysis of resource development, the second part of the thesis, I emphasize that the words "resource development" have been chosen with some deliberateness. Richard L. Meier defines a resource as "an opportunity in the environment that has been identified and appraised by a population of potential users."[13] Using his definition, I suggest that resource development would mean no more than the widening of the range of choices or opportunities in an environment to an increasing number of people. Strictly defined, such opportunities are limited to those found in the primary productive activities of agriculture, forestry, fishing, and

[13] Richard L. Meier, "Resource Planning," *International Encyclopedia of the Social Sciences*, p. 137.

mining. However, there is no reason why the definition cannot be extended to cover all productive activities including trading, transportation, and manufacturing.

The important point to stress—and this is where the element of deliberateness comes in—is that resource development is not the same thing as economic development. The former may or may not lead to the latter. The position, I believe, is well put by Myint in his description of the effect of export crop production in developing countries.

> Peasant export [crop] production expanded without the introduction of radical improvements in the agricultural techniques used in subsistence production, ... when the peasants took to "specializing" in export crops, it merely meant that they were devoting the whole of their resources to export production. In doing this, they took full advantage of the *market opportunities* available to them, but this does not mean that they took full advantage of the *technical opportunities* to improve their productivity ... the same combination of land, labour and capital [have] been used throughout half a century of rapid [agricultural] expansion.[14]

Other writers have commented on this possible lack of congruence between resource development and economic development in underdeveloped countries. Gunnar Myrdal, in his brilliant exposition, stated that,

> In South Asia, the processes of capital accumulation and spread were frustrated. The plantations, like the mines, remained enclaves in largely stagnant economies while the initial impulses failed to trigger cumulative and self-perpetuating growth. The

14 H. Myint, *The Economics of Developing Countries* (London: Hutchinson, 1964), p. 51. (Italics added.)

promising beginning in agriculture did not spill over into other sectors; a generally dynamic response failed to materialise. In short, the subsequent development in South Asia continued to be what Boeke has aptly referred to as "static expansion."[15]

Myrdal suggested that part of the reason for this phenomenon of "static expansion" in the economy of South Asian countries is the fact that new income or profits generated are invariably lost to the countries concerned through remittances abroad or their being spent on imported commodities. Seldom are they used to stimulate increased demand for locally produced goods. In such a situation, traditional things are left to be produced largely in traditional ways with no concern for per unit cost reduction or increased productivity per man.

Resource development may or may not lead to economic development. The distinction, I am aware, may in part be simply a function of time and of our present inadequate understanding of the process of cumulative economic change. However, the real problem that needs to be examined further concerns the conditions which facilitate the identification of those opportunities or resources that need to be developed in the environment. Such identifications tend to be innovative in character and to that extent raise the question of how far regional mobility stimulates innovative activity.

REGIONAL MOBILITY AND INNOVATIVE ACTIVITY

Frederick J. Teggart, the American historian, insists that the "great advances of mankind have been due, not to the mere aggregation, assemblage, or acquisition of disparate ideas, but to the emergence of a certain type

---

[15] Gunnar Myrdal, *Asian Drama: An Inquiry into the Poverty of Nations*, vol. 1 (New York: Twentieth Century Fund, 1968), p. 448.

of mental activity which is set up by the opposition of different idea systems."[16] New ideas, according to him, arise only when the clash of ideas provokes comparisons and critical discussions of the differences. The individual is thereby released from the trammels of tradition and is able to express himself in the organization of new customs. Teggart remarks that for this reason migrations and collisions of groups of people have been essential for the genesis of new ideas. Only in this way can there be the "break-up of crystallized systems of organization and of thought" that is necessary for real cultural advance.

Teggart's position can be criticized as extreme on two counts: it places too much emphasis on the importance of friction and social disruption for the emergence of new ideas, and it conceives of real innovations as always epoch-making.

In his extremely thorough study, H. G. Barnett accepts the basic element of Teggart's theory, that the "apposition of alternate values, things, and usages can bring about an entirely new concept that is qualitatively distinct from either of the alternatives. Furthermore, the conjunction of such differences can be a stimulus for the emergence of some new idea deriving from them. The difference itself induces change."[17] For this reason, Barnett concludes that any custom that encourages the mingling of people with variant habits provides an opportunity for a mutual appraisal of their differences and therefore for innovative activities. Among such customs, he lists the role of the market place in both modern and primitive societies, as well as the presence of itinerant or resident traders in foreign lands. These traders, by

16 Frederick J. Teggart, *The Processes of History* (New Haven, Conn.: Yale University Press, 1918), p. 112.

17 H. G. Barnett, *Innovation: The Basis of Cultural Change* (New York: McGraw-Hill, 1953), p. 46.

their very nature, are instruments for the presentation of contrasts, if not in their behaviour, then certainly in the wares that they import. Other circumstances which encourage innovative activities include inter-ethnic marriages, exchange of ambassadors, emigration and expatriation, slavery and wage-labour recruitment among foreign populations, exploration and adventure, and finally, conquest and colonization.

Although Barnett defines innovation in terms of its qualitative difference from existing forms in resource development, I submit that the distinction between qualitative reorganization and quantitative variation is less important in determining an innovation. A mere introduction of objects or ideas from one area to another would qualify as an innovation if such an action had innovative results, that is, if it led to an increase in productive opportunities in the area.

Furthermore, in order to relate regional mobility to resource development, I would like also to explore Barnett's description of the mechanics of innovative activity. According to him, all cultural changes are initiated by individuals. The stimulus for a new idea or a new behaviour is consequently always specific to a given individual. Nonetheless, conditions external to the individual do have a marked effect upon his innovative potential and upon the potential of the group in which he lives. Of the various eternal conditions which Barnett lists, two are of special significance for our purpose. The first is the failure of authoritative controls. Barnett convincingly argues that much of the process of socialization in any society is an authoritarian device to make individuals conform to norms and accept the values and standards of their society. In periods of social and political upheaval when such controls collapse, or in moving to a foreign land where they do not exist, the way is open to innovative activities.

Barnett describes the reason for this phenomenon. "The effect of all such situations in which there is an abandonment or a withdrawal of authoritative controls is to cut the individual adrift from his moorings. He loses his orientation points, and he must take new bearings in order not to drift aimlessly and anxiously. The microcosm in which he has lived has been destructuralized and is not habitable in that condition. He strains to give it some organization and some meaning, and in so doing he innovates or accepts the definition of the situation offered by others. Or, still more often, he and his associates work out a solution together."[18]

Another of the external conditions stimulating innovative activities on the part of individuals or groups of individuals, Barnett refers to as "the deprivation of essentials."[19] The word "essentials" in this context he regards as an entirely relative term having significance only for a particular group. It is something which such a group considers vital for its survival or for the preservation of customs and modes of living which it greatly values. From this point of view, essentials are strongly culturally determined and highly particularistic. The type of innovation caused by deprivation of such essentials is sometimes no more than a revival or borrowing of old ideas to meet a crisis. These are nonetheless innovative because their re-establishment out of their geographical or historical context almost invariably involves some modification, if only to make them fit in with current ideas and styles of living.

Migration, land alienation, and forced or voluntary

18 Ibid., p. 72.
19 Ibid., p. 80.

alteration of the economic base of a people often create a sense of deprivation and stimulate innovative cultural readjustments if such a people are to survive. At the very least, adjustments must be made to accommodate for the absence of essentials that were relied upon in the old habitat. Barnett suggests that the reason why innovation appears with deprivation is similar to that given for the failure of authoritative controls; namely, a familiar universe of associations and sanctions has been distorted or destroyed and must be reorganized. The wrenching away of any control mechanism, including the natural environment, requires a reorientation. Unsettlement for any cause creates a fluid situation in which the old values are no longer operative. With the old sanctions and compulsions gone or of doubtful validity, the way is open for the creation and the acceptance of new interpretations.

In resource development, therefore, it is not only innovative objects or traits that command attention. Institutions, organizations, or arrangements which make possible the sustained exploitation of resources by individuals or groups of individuals are of equal significance. Regional mobility, since it implies crossing ethnic or national boundaries, can be assumed to give rise to a high degree of unsettlement due to the withdrawal of authoritative controls and deprivation of essentials. It can therefore be expected to stimulate innovative activities for purposes of resource development.

Conclusion

In the study of regional mobility, the focus should concentrate more on the individual and group responses to the dislocation resulting from a transfer of residences, especially when this transfer involves moving into other countries or into the lands of other ethnic groups. These responses often have innovative implications whether in terms of organization, techniques of production, introduction of material goods, or diffusion of social values. However, the effectiveness of these innovations in terms of resource development and the extent to which they facilitate the assimilation of the immigrant groups is seriously affected by the social and economic conditions subsisting at the time. In this respect, I distinguish broadly between conditions in pre-industrial and industrial societies and, in the West African situation, between conditions before and after the attainment of national independence.

The basic thesis remains that migrants, because of their experience and the very special circumstances of their stay abroad, make real and significant contributions to resource development both in the lands of their foreign sojourn and in their home areas.

CHAPTER II:
PATTERN AND MAGNITUDE OF REGIONAL MOBILITY

IN HIS STUDY, *Economics of Migration*, Julius Isaac provides a fourfold classification of human movements in the mass. This comprises invasion, conquest, colonization, and migration. He defines invasion as "the thrust of a primitive and virile people from its own territory into that of a more highly developed State."[1] The movement may go on for some generations before the group settles down permanently, and its success often depends on the sheer number of invaders or their use of force. In the case of conquest, the situation is reversed. A well-developed state uses its technical and organizational superiority to subjugate relatively backward peoples and incorporates their territory into its own political system. The whole operation may not involve a large number of people from the advanced country, but could result in a mass movement of people from the conquered territory.

Two types of colonization movements can be distinguished: exploitation and settlement. Exploitation occurs as a result of the initiative of a state or its substitutes and involves the transfer of a relatively small number of businessmen, administrators, and soldiers to supervise the peaceful exploitation of the land and resources of the colonized people. Colonization of the

---

[1] Julius Isaac, *Economics of Migration* (London: Kegan Paul, 1947), pp. 1-3.

settlement type occurs, according to Henry P. Fairchild, when a "well-established, progressive, and physically vigorous State sends out bodies of citizens, officially as a rule, to settle in certain specified localities. The regions chosen are newly discovered or thinly settled countries, where the native inhabitants are so few, or are on such an inferior stage of culture that they offer but slight resistance to the entrance of the colonists."[2]

The fourth type of movement is migration. This, Isaac emphasized, may be either forced or free. Forced migration is an involuntary transfer of people such as is involved in slave trading or the deportation of convicts or undesirable aliens. Free migration, on the other hand, is the voluntary movement of free individuals from one area to another with the intention of a permanent change in residence.

In the previous chapter, I indicated that the emphasis on the intention of permanent residential change makes the concept of migration rather restrictive for our purpose. And the concept is inadequate to convey the complexity of mobility in Africa today. R. Mansell Prothero has offered us a somewhat comprehensive typology of African mobility.[3] First, he distinguishes between economic and non-economic migratory movements (fig. 1). Of the non-economic movements, he lists the movements of pilgrims, especially Muslim pilgrims to Mecca, as well as those of political and ethnic refugees. And in order to appreciate fully the complexity of the pilgrimage movement, I should stress that until very recently this was a

[2] Henry P. Fairchild, *Immigration: A World Movement and Its American Significance*, rev. ed. (New York: Macmillan, 1925), p. 19.

[3] R. Mansell Prothero, "A Typology of African Mobility" (Seminar Paper, Department of Geography, University of Liverpool, 1967).

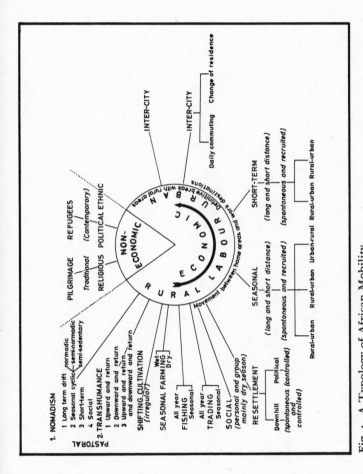

Fig. 1. A Typology of African Mobility

SOURCE: R. Mansell Prothero, "A Typology of African Mobility" (Seminar Paper, De-partment of Geography, University of Liverpool, November 1967).

stage-by-stage movement in which a pilgrim gradually worked his way to Mecca, stopping to work for months or years at different places on the way. It is reckoned, for instance, that such hopeful pilgrims from West Africa make up nearly 25 per cent of the workers in the Gezira cotton fields in the Republic of Sudan.[4]

Of the economic movements, Prothero distinguishes those of pastoralists, fishermen, farmers, and traders. The pastoralists engage in long-term, seasonal-cyclic, or short-term nomadic movements. In hilly or mountainous areas, their movements may be in the nature of trans-humance involving upward and downward movements during different seasons of the year. The fishermen cover long distances either seasonally or all year round to escape the congestion or depletion of the fishing in their home area. The farmers, under the impact of the deleterious effect of shifting cultivation or overpopulation, or because of the seasonal rhythm of farm work, traverse long distances in search of new lands or new employment opportunities in agriculture. The traders search for sales opportunities and their enterprise carries them far away from home.

Although all these movements in West Africa have a history going far back into the past, the colonial regime has served to magnify and distort their relative significance. The magnification has arisen because the number of people involved in these movements today is greater than ever before; the distortion occurs because a large proportion of those moving consists simply of seasonal or short-term agricultural labour. Indeed, re-

---

[4] I. A. Hassoun, " 'Western' Migration and Settlement in the Gezira," *Sudan Notes and Records*, 33, pt. 1 (June 1952): 60-112; D. B. Mather, "Migration in the Sudan," *Geographical Essays on British Tropical Lands*, eds. R. W. Steel and C. A. Fisher (London: George Phillip & Son, 1956), pp. 113-44; and H. R. J. Davies, "The West African in the Economic Geography of Sudan," *Geography*, 49 (1964): 222-35.

cent concern with the magnitude of migration of agricultural labour has tended to distract attention from the
historically well-established and more diverse types of
movements still going on all over West Africa. And it is
these movements that have a more important significance
for resource development than what is currently attri-
buted to them.

Let me emphasize that I am not primarily interested
in the colonial labour movement. A number of studies
of this movement, especially in the last decade, have
been undertaken and are available to anyone who wishes
to examine this topic. My discussion of it simply provides a perspective for my primary interest—the movement of free, enterprising individuals throughout West
Africa from the past to the present.

BACKGROUND TO THE COLONIAL LABOUR MIGRATIONS

The history of the colonial labour migrations in West
Africa dates from the early decades of the present century. After almost three centuries of the slave trade, the
European in West Africa was gradually coerced or per-
suaded by his home government to switch his line of
trade from slaves to the natural produce of the land.
The change had a compelling economic advantage: the
new industrial complexes in Europe at the time were
stimulating an almost insatiable demand for a variety
of agricultural raw materials. In particular, oilseeds
were in great demand. Vegetable oil was proving vitally
important both for maintaining the industrial machines
in good condition and for conversion into a wide variety
of products.

The physical environment in West Africa tolerated
the growth of a large number of oilseeds of different
kinds (fig. 2). The environment divides broadly into
two types: forests in the south, extending for nearly one

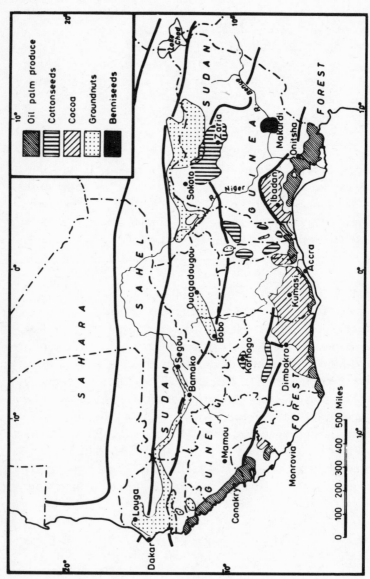

Fig. 2. West Africa: Oilseed-producing Areas

hundred miles inland, and grasslands to the north stretching for nearly a thousand miles up to the border of the Sahara Desert. Three broad belts are distinguished: the Guinea, the Sudan, and the Sahel Savanna in that order from south to north. Generally, the height of grasses and the density of trees fall from the Guinea to the Sahel Savanna.

Other characteristics of these belts of vegetation need not concern us here. What is important from our point of view is that in each belt oilseeds of one type or the other can be grown. In the forest environment, these oilseeds are produced by perennial trees, notably the oil palm and cocoa. The oil palm is native to the West African forest, but cocoa was introduced into the area only in the last quarter of the nineteenth century. In the Guinea Savanna, the shea tree is a native oilseed plant, but more recently benniseed and soyabeans have been introduced. In the Sudan and Sahel Savanna, groundnuts or peanuts and cottonseeds have also been grown since the distant past.

The exploitation of this agricultural produce for the European markets dominated the economy of West Africa throughout the colonial period. However, from the beginning the evacuation of these commodities from the interior to the coast posed a number of serious problems. Unlike slaves, who were expected to get to the coast on foot, the movement of produce required transportation. It is thus no accident that the prelude to the colonial domination of West Africa by European powers was the exploration and discovery of its rivers and waterways (fig. 3). Between 1775 and 1870, the travels of intrepid explorers such as Mungo Park, Hugh Clapperton, the Lander brothers, Heinrich Barth, a German, and Réné Caille, a Frenchman, did much to lay bare the natural transportation potentials of West Africa.

45

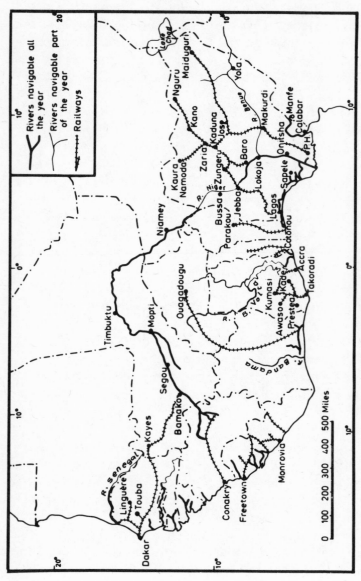

Fig. 3. West Africa: Waterways and Railways

What these explorers revealed, however, was far from satisfactory. The most important river of the area, namely the Niger, has a most peculiar course. It rises close to the coast on the Fouta Jallon Highlands near the Sierra Leone-Guinea boundary. For the first 700 miles, it proceeds towards the desert, then it turns eastward for another 1,000 miles and eventually southwards to enter the sea in a delta in Nigeria. Apart from the Niger, there are the other rivers of the Benue, the Volta, the Bandama, and the Senegal which, although having more direct routes to the coast, suffered from one disability or the other. When it is not the existence of falls and cataracts along their courses, it may be their highly fluctuating regimes and deltaic mouths. Their greatest disability, however, is that they all flow through regions which are by and large sparsely populated.

The implication of these various facts is clear. Any large-scale exploitation of the resources of West Africa could not rely on the rivers for the evacuation of the produce. Given the level of technological development in Europe by the second half of the nineteenth century, the alternative was also clear. Railways had to be constructed and harbour facilities improved. Both these decisions involved the investment of a sizeable amount of capital which could not be provided by any single small European trading company in West Africa at the time. At any rate, whoever provided the capital would have to exercise a certain degree of political and administrative control to ensure that the investment was allowed to generate the anticipated output of commodities. The results were the partitioning of West Africa by European powers into trading spheres of influence, the beginning and development of rail lines, and the eventual administrative control and domination of the region.

I am aware that in this brief sketch I have done less

than justice to the fascinating history of the "scramble for Africa." But then the exposition of this period of West African history is not my immediate concern. What I am anxious to emphasize is the role that the transportation network came to play in the pattern and magnitude of the colonial labour movement. Throughout West Africa, the crucial node in the colonial transportation network was the port. All rail lines started inland from the port and all roads led to the port. Great cost and profit advantage accrued to any producer who operated close to the port; the reverse was the lot of a producer who lived far away from the coast and the ports. In other words, with European colonization, coastal areas became economically the most important parts of West Africa.

This twentieth-century development represented a reversal of historical values. Civilization, it has been said, came to West Africa from the north. Even if one challenges the historical validity of this assertion, it is still true that the most highly developed empires and kingdoms in West Africa were to be found in the Sudan Savanna areas in the interior. Apart from the well-known empires of Ghana, Mali, and Songhai, there were the Tekrur kingdom in the west, the Mossi kingdoms, and the various Hausa states. The presence of these political and administrative organizations meant one thing: a basic pax or polity was established under which producers and traders could engage in profitable activities. It did not matter whether this pax was often or sporadically disturbed. What was important was the fact of its existence; this made possible the concentration of a fairly large population in these interior areas of West Africa from at least the early middle ages. Although representing present-day distribution, figure 4 gives some idea of these interior areas of population concentration (figs. 4 and 5).

48

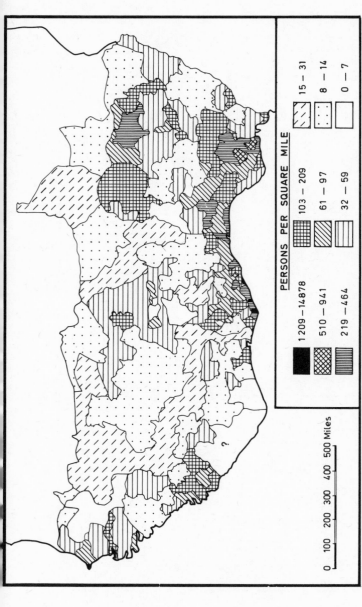

PERSONS PER SQUARE MILE

1 209 – 14 878	103 – 209	15 – 31
510 – 941	61 – 97	8 – 14
219 – 464	32 – 59	0 – 7

0 100 200 300 400 500 Miles

Fig. 4. West Africa: Population Distribution *c.* 1950. Most of the dense concentration of population dates from the period of European activity on the West Coast.

SOURCE: W. B. Morgan and J. C. Pugh, *West Africa* (London: Methuen, 1969), p. 8.

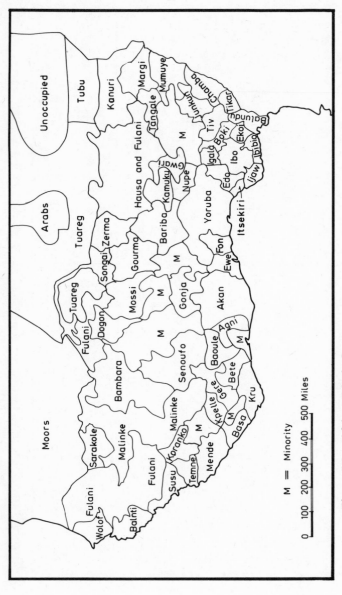

Fig. 5. West Africa: Ethnic Groups

SOURCE: W. B. Morgan and J. C. Pugh, *West Africa* (London: Methuen, 1969), p. 16.

By contrast, the forest area to the south was essentially backward and sparsely settled. Parts of it in Nigeria, the western Ivory Coast, and Liberia even today have very little population. Historically, the forest area served more as a refuge zone for numerous, small, poorly organized ethnic groups, forced to flee in the face of more powerful neighbours. It is true, of course, that some impressive state developments also took place within the forest belt. Some of the best known of these include the Benin, the Yoruba, the Abomey, and the Ashanti kingdoms. In most of these cases, however, there are indications that these states were the product of the colonizing adventures of immigrant groups from the north. Moreover, it is also true that in parts of the forest belt, notably in the Ibo area of Nigeria, high densities of rural population occur which cannot easily be explained as the product of migration into the area.

Nonetheless, it was on this historical pattern of population distribution that the colonial economy of export agriculture came to be imposed. The relatively empty forest lands which were nearer the coast and the ports became the scene of intense economic activities. Apart from the oilseed plants such as the oil palm, coconuts, and cocoa, these areas were given over to the cultivation of coffee, banana, kolanuts, and rubber. Moreover, they provided valuable tropical hardwood timber for export. Large areas of land, used only marginally in the past, were taken over by European planters and African farmers in the former French West African colonies. The evacuation of the annually increasing agricultural output required the construction of not only the railway from 1885 onwards but also a dense network of roads. Especially after the 1920s, the significance of road transportation in the forest belt became paramount. Along the routes through which the export commodities were evacuated, a wide variety of manufactured goods from Europe was moved as return freight. The effect was gradually to change the style and standard of living in these areas and to provide increasingly significant incentives for rapid resource development.

By contrast, the extensive grassland areas in the interior, covering three-quarters of West Africa, had relatively few export crops to provide. These consisted largely of groundnuts, cotton, cottonseeds and, to a lesser extent, benniseed, and soyabeans. In a few places, notably Jos in Nigeria, there were also some minerals to export. The crucial problem was the evacuation of even this limited quantity. The major colonial powers in West Africa attempted to extend the railway from different coastal points to tap this interior heartland. The French, in fact, had an ambitious project for a railway network comprising four main lines starting from Dakar, Conakry, Abidjan, and Cotonou and converging on the river Niger. Two of these lines—from Dakar and Conakry—did reach the Niger. The others remained far from this objective. The British were more limited in their goals and seemed to give priority to rail development in areas where immediate prospects of economic returns were bright. Thus, only the lines within Nigeria penetrated any considerable distance inland. The Ghana lines were confined to the forest belt and so was the single Sierra Leone line. No attempt was made to build any line in the Gambia. The river Gambia was regarded as adequate for the needs of that colony.

Perhaps more important from the point of view of the interior areas were the transportation policies pursued by the various colonial governments. Because the railways represented such an enormous investment of public capital from the metropolitan country, every attempt was made to dampen any competition with them for traffic from the interior. Little was done to provide direct road links between these areas and the coast. Only roads serving as feeders to the railways were constructed.

The implication of this pattern of transportation development was clear. The interior of West Africa was an area of high transport costs. The farmer here received low prices for his agricultural produce because of the extra transport costs still needed to evacuate this to the ports. On the other hand, he had to pay exceedingly high prices for imported manufactured goods which had to be brought to him from the coast. It is no surprise therefore that people in these historically important areas in the interior of West Africa found themselves at a great economic disadvantage in the colonial period. To correct this, a large number found recourse in migrating to the more prosperous farms and plantations in the south.

What made such movement easy to contemplate for most of the people was the fact that it involved minimal disruption to the basic economic activity in their home area. The background to this state of affairs is to be found in the character of the climate of West Africa. Not only does total annual rainfall decrease from over one hundred inches on the coast to about twenty inches at the northernmost limits, but the period of dry season increases correspondingly in the same direction. Thus, for most of the interior grassland areas, the dry season lasts from five to seven months each year. The early part of the dry season, usually from September to November, is the major harvesting period. The end of the season, starting from about March, is the time for preparing the land. The long, slack period in between, that is, from December to March, provides an invaluable opportunity to earn extra income each year by migrating to the farms and plantations in the forested south.

This geographical background makes it easy to appreciate the broad pattern and characteristics of the colonial labour movement (fig. 6). This is, in general, a movement of people from north to south, and most of the migration is of a seasonal character, although a migrant may return each season to the same farm or plantation. A large proportion of the migrants have no skill or expertise other than in farming and can seek wage employment only as labourers or farm hands. Most of these migrants are young adult males largely in the age group of twenty to thirty-four years.

A survey of migrants into Ghana and the Ivory Coast organized jointly by the statistics or research division of the governments of the Ivory Coast, Ghana, Upper Volta, Niger, Togo, and Dahomey represents the best documentation of these movements to date.[5] The survey lasted from March 1958 to March 1959. It was conducted at specific crossing points where, it was reckoned, diverse routes taken by migrants converged. These comprised, in the Ivory Coast, the major road and rail junction town of Bouake; in Ghana, the ferry crossing towns of Yeji, Bamboi, and Otisu. At the Togo-Ghana frontier, five posts, Aflao, Batoume, Noépé, Kpadafe, Klouto, and Badou, were chosen to tap any migrants from Togo, Dahomey, and Nigeria.

The survey revealed that some four hundred thousand to five hundred thousand persons moved into these two countries over the one-year period. The major ethnic groups concerned were largely those from the north. Sixty per cent came from the Voltaic group with the

[5] Most of the data used have been taken from the working document for the symposium, "Study of Migrations in West Africa," CCTA/CSA, Joint Project no. 3, MIG (61) 2, January 1961. See also Jean Rouch, "Migrations au Ghana (Enquête 1953-55)," *Journal de la Société des Africanistes*, 26, fasc. 1 and 2 (1956): 33-196.

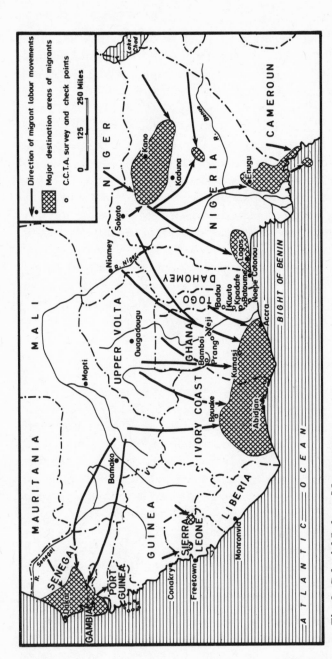

Fig. 6. Colonial Labour Movements

SOURCE: R. Mansell Prothero, "Migrant Labour in West Africa," *Journal of Local Administration Overseas*, 1, no. 3 (July 1962): 151.

Mossi people of Upper Volta predominating. (See fig. 5 for the areas occupied by the various ethnic groups.) Another 13 per cent comprised members of the Mande groups, notably Bambara, Diula, and Malinke. Ten per cent consisted of the Niger group, mainly Hausa, Zerma and Peulhs (Fulani). All in all, nearly 85 per cent of those entering these two countries came from the north.

The survey also showed that over 80 per cent of the migrants stayed for less than a year at a time. Seven per cent stayed for up to two years; 4 per cent for up to five years; another 4 per cent stayed over five years; and 3 per cent made no response. However, of the migrants, 25 per cent made only one trip in the year; 59 per cent made between two and four trips; and 14 per cent made over four trips. As would be expected, the trader groups, notably the Hausa and Zerma, made the greatest number of trips and repeated short stays. The agricultural labour groups, such as the Mossi and Senoufo, made less frequent trips but stayed for relatively longer periods.

The educational background of the migrants is revealing. Seventy-five to 80 per cent of them were illiterate; 10 to 15 per cent had attended Koranic schools, and barely 2 to 5 per cent had attended Western-type schools. As was also to be expected, nearly 50 per cent of them were employed as agricultural labourers; about 20 per cent operated as traders; and between 15 and 25 per cent were engaged in unspecified occupations.

The demographic characteristics of the migrants are no less interesting: West African migration is essentially a male phenomenon; 92 per cent of those surveyed were men. Most of the migrants were young, some 75 per cent being in the age group 20 to 34 years. Many, about 52 per cent, were single, and the majority of those married travelled without their wives.

Nonetheless, the figure of 400,000 to 500,000 immigrants does little justice to the total number of people involved in this colonial labour movement. In the first place, it does not take account of the movement into other territories apart from Ghana and the Ivory Coast. Senegal, for instance, had its *navétanes* or "strange-farmers" who since 1946 were said to number between 40,000 to 45,000 a year.[6] Other countries, notably the Gambia, Sierra Leone, and Nigeria reported such immigrants, although their number is not easily available.[7] In the second place, this figure ignores an equally sizeable number of movements within countries which extend from the coast far into the interior. For instance, R. Mansell Prothero reported a census carried out from October 1952 to March 1953 in Nigeria which indicated that some 259,000 people were involved in southward migration through Sokoto Province alone.[8] Seventy-three per cent of these originated in Sokoto Province, another 10 per cent came from other parts of Northern Nigeria, whilst the remaining 17 per cent were from the neighbouring French territory of Niger. If Sokoto Province alone recorded over a quarter of a million such migrants, it is no exaggeration to suggest that probably a million people are involved in these movements within Nigeria.

All in all, then, it can be asserted that probably two million people were involved in these colonial migratory labour movements from the northern to the southern parts of West Africa. The large number means, in effect, that they have overshadowed the older type of movements comprising mainly those of traders, farmers in search of new lands, and fishermen extending their

6 Virginia Thompson and Richard Adloff, *French West Africa* (London: Allen & Unwin, 1958), p. 493.

7 H. Reginald Jarrett, "The Strange Farmers of the Gambia," *Geographical Review*, 39, no. 4 (October 1949): 649-57.

8 Prothero, "Migratory Labour from North-Western Nigeria," *Africa*, 27, no. 3 (July 1957): 251-61.

fishing grounds further afield. Since, however, the movement of traders was recorded in the 1958-59 survey, it
may be interesting to investigate how different their
pattern and characteristics were from those of the agricultural labour. Jean Rouch, the French ethnographer,
in his contribution to the survey indicated that of the
three hundred thousand to four hundred thousand
people coming into Ghana alone, only fifty thousand to
eighty thousand or less than 20 per cent were traders.

THE TRAVELLING TRADER OF WEST AFRICA

What was most striking about the trader-migrants in
this survey was the dominance of a few ethnic groups.
These are the Bambara-Soninke, the Zerma, the Hausa-
Fulani, and the Yoruba. The survey revealed that 65 per
cent of trader-migrants came from these four groups.
Furthermore, among these groups, there was a greater
tendency for frequent trips in and out of the area and
for repeated short stays. The trader-migrants tended to
be slightly older than the average and to be married. Of
the married migrants, the Zerma and Hausa had the
greatest numbers of "temporarily single" men. The
Yoruba, on the other hand, travelled more often with
their wives. The result is that 22 per cent of their number is accounted for by women, as against an average of
8 per cent for the survey as a whole.

A question that immediately arises is why the class of
trader-migrants is dominated by such a small number of
ethnic groups? Some aspects of the answer to this question become obvious when we consider the historical
characteristics of these groups in greater detail.

The Bambara-Soninke belong to the major ethnic
group distinguished by George Murdock as the Nuclear
Mande. This is the group to which he ascribes not only
the invention of agriculture in the Sudan but also other

vital cultural roles in the history of West Africa. When the Arabs first arrived on the fringes of the Western Sudan in the eleventh century, they found the Soninke organized in a powerful state known as Ghana, with its capital near Oualata in modern Mali. Trade with the Berbers of Morocco had already been well established by then and had stimulated the development of hand-icraft manufactures, the growth of mercantile towns, and eventually the evolution of complex political in-stitutions. Murdock emphasizes that among the Nuclear Mande, "trade assumes substantial proportions every-where, and regular markets are apparently universal. Commerce with the northeast is largely monopolised by the Nono (whose principal city is Djenne) and with the Atlantic Coast by the Susu, whereas the Diula and Marka, mercantile branches of the Soninke, conduct most of the trade that flows east, north and south."[9]

The important point to stress about the Bambara-Soninke is the fact that they are people among whom there has been a long tradition of trading and urban-ization. Indeed, it is these two characteristics that distinguish all the groups listed as mainly traders in the survey report. The Zerma, for instance, are part of the Songhaic groups of people who founded one of the suc-cessor empires to that of Ghana. From their chief city of Niamey on the Niger, these people also played a prominent part in the trans-Saharan trade, especially as the Moroccan intrusion into the Songhai area in the sixteenth century forced the trade to shift to more easter-ly routes. The Hausa are well known for their highly developed specialized handicraft manufactures, for their prominent role in both the trans-Saharan and the intra-regional trade, for their political organization into seven

9 George D. Murdock, *Africa: Its Peoples and Their Culture History* (New York: McGraw-Hill, 1959), p. 74.

states, and for their metropolitan cities such as Kano, Katsina, Gobir, and Zaria. The position among the Yoruba is also well documented.[10] They stand out clearly as the most urbanized ethnic group within tropical Africa. Their urbanization, apart from having arisen as a technique of colonization, was clearly sustained by extensive trading relations among themselves and between them and neighbouring ethnic groups.

During the colonial period, the trading venturesomeness of these various groups was given a new impetus. This arose as a direct result of improved transporation and indirectly because the economy of their cities had been undermined such that they needed to find new sources of economic support.[11] The establishment of a modern transportation network imposed a new pattern of spatial integration and generated a new system of cities for the export-oriented economy of the colonial period. In areas such as the former Eastern Nigeria and the Middle Belt where there were very few traditional cities, new centres grew up to serve as crucial nodes for this economy. They included places like Port Harcourt, Aba, Umuahia, Enugu, Makurdi, Jos, and Kaduna. All these towns are today less than seventy years old. By contrast, in the Hausa and Yoruba areas of the country where there was a well-developed system of traditional cities, only those cities on the new transport routes showed any evidence of sustained growth. Most of the others not

10 See, for example, William R. Bascom, "Urbanization Among the Yoruba," *American Journal of Sociology*, 60, no. 5 (1955): 446-54; Akin L. Mabogunje, *Yoruba Towns* (Ibadan, Nigeria: Ibadan University Press, 1962); Peter C. Lloyd, Akin L. Mabogunje, and B. Awe, eds., *The City of Ibadan* (Cambridge: Cambridge University Press, 1967); and Eva Krapf-Askari, *Yoruba Towns and Cities: An Enquiry into the Nature of Urban Social Phenomena* (Oxford: At the Clarendon Press, 1969).

11 The following discussion is taken from Akin L. Mabogunje, *Urbanization in Nigeria* (London: University of London Press, 1968).

situated on the new routes found their economy undermined, and large numbers of their people had to emi-
grate to seek their fortunes elsewhere.

Yorubaland further exemplifies the consequences of
this development. Many of the urban centres that found
themselves no longer functional in the new economy
were not just small, insignificant towns but some of the
important traditional metropolises. These included the
large cities of the Oyo Empire such as Ogbomosho,
Ejigbo, Ede, Shaki, Iseyin, Iwo, and even Oyo, the old
capital itself. People from these cities had to move out
to other places to trade. The most curious fact is that a
large proportion of them went to Ghana, the Ivory Coast,
Upper Volta, and Mali. The officials who organized the
1952 Census of Nigeria tried to obtain special returns
on the number and whereabouts of these migrants in
respect to the two towns of Ogbomosho and Ejigbo. In
1952, Ogbomosho had a population of 139,535; it recorded 5,820 persons in the Gold Coast and 12,895 elsewhere, making a total of 18,715 or nearly 13 per cent of
its population. Of this, roughly one-third were adult
males, another third adult females, and the remaining
third children. Ejigbo had a population in 1952 of 15,851,
apart from 8,692 or 56 per cent who were in Ghana or
the Ivory Coast. Again the distribution among adult
males, adult females, and children was roughly of the
same order.[12]

Although similar figures are not available for the traditional urban centres in the Mande, Zerma, or the Hausa
areas, there is evidence of a non-quantitative nature
to emphasize that experiences in these towns are not
greatly dissimilar from those in the Yoruba country. In

12 Nigeria, Department of Statistics, *Population Census of the Western
Region of Nigeria: 1952* (Ibadan: Government Printer, 1956), p. 10.

other words, for this type of regional mobility in West Africa, the colonial regime served both directly and indirectly to further stimulate an increase in volume and intensity. But, unlike the colonial labour movement whose pattern was roughly north to south or from the interior to the coast, the pattern of this traditionally based mobility was more complex. Already, we have mentioned that the Bambara-Soninke traders travel east, north, and south of their home region. The Zerma move to the west and southwest. The Hausa spread across the grassland zone of West Africa, whilst the Yoruba are found to the west, north, and northwest of their territory.

Some evidence of the antiquity of these movements may be in order at this stage. It would seem that among the Mande-speaking traders (Malinke, Bambara, Diula, and Soninke) the increasing demand in North Africa and Europe for gold in the latter half of the fourteenth century was the occasion for their widespread movements eastward and southward away from their home base. Ivor Wilks, for instance, regards their movement "into the Jenne area as probably part of a wider movement that took others into the Hausa lands of what is now Northern Nigeria."[13] According to the *Kano Chronicle*, the Mande-speaking traders were responsible for the introduction of Islam into the Hausa country in the second half of the fourteenth century.[14] Mande traders who migrated southward about the same time were also known to have founded or to have helped to found new towns in the territories of other ethnic groups. Among the Bobo, they founded the town of Bobo-Dioulasso in modern Upper Volta, fifteen days' journey south of Jenne; among the Senoufo, they founded Begho in

13 Ivor Wilks, "A Medieval Trade-Route from the Niger to the Gulf of Guinea," *Journal of African History*, 3, no. 2 (1962): 337-38.
14 H. R. Palmer, trans., *The Kano Chronicle, Journal of the Royal Anthropological Institute*, 38 (1908): 70.

modern Ghana, yet another fifteen days south of Kong.
All these towns became important staging posts for the
caravans plying between the Jenne region and Begho.
Wilks suggests that the colonization of Begho marked
the southernmost limit of permanent Mande settlement.
Subsequent groups moving further south simply attached themselves to existing towns. There appears to have
been, for example, a movement of Diula traders to
Dormaa (or Wam) about forty-five miles south of Begho
in the sixteenth century, while the Sarakole appear to
have had offshoots as far south as Nkoranza in modern
Ghana. Indeed, Duarte Pacheco Pereira mentioned that
there were already Mande traders on the Ghana coast
in the Elmina area when the Portuguese arrived there
in 1471.[15]

Similarly, there is evidence of considerable movement
of Hausas to southern Ghana through Djougou, Nikki,
Yendi, and Salaga well before the colonial period. It is
certainly of this route that Leo Africanus spoke in the
sixteenth century when he described the merchants of
the Hausa State of Guangara (Katsina-Laka) as "travel-
ling into the aforesaid region abounding with gold,
because the ways are so rough and difficult that their
camels cannot go upon them, they carry their wares
upon slaves' backs; who being laden with great burdens
do usually travel ten or twelve miles a day."[16] And Jack
Goody suggests that it is an indication of the relative
importance of this route that the first maps to present
"detailed information about the Akan hinterland" or
southern Ghana early in the eighteenth century (that

15 Duarte Pacheco Pereira, *Esmeraldo de Situ Orbis*, trans. and ed.
George H. T. Kimble; Hakluyt Society Publications, vol. 79 (London:
John Murray, 1937), p. 120.
16 Leo Africanus, *The History and Description of Africa*, ed. Robert
Brown and trans. John Pory, vol. 3; Hakluyt Society Publications, vol.
94 (London, 1896), p. 832.

is, those of Delisle in 1722 and Rennell in 1790) were "both clearly derive[d] from travellers who journeyed down the road from Hausaland."[17] It is also to these routes that Joseph Dupuis referred when he wrote, "The two last roads are sometimes called the old roads, from their antiquity and pre-eminence" and again, "the NE [route] is mainly the track of amity and alliance, and this, which is one of the most beaten roads in Africa, the Ashantees travel over without scruple, but mostly in the society of Muslims, to Salgha [Salaga], Tonoma [Eastern Dagomba], Ghamba [Gambaga], Yandy [Yendi] and other parts of Daghomba."[18]

Evidence of the trading activities of the Yoruba is more difficult to come by until the nineteenth century. Clapperton, for instance, described Yoruba traders as being well into the Nupe country to the north in 1825. He found no fewer than twenty-one of them, mainly women, living in his landlady's house at one time.[19] Nonetheless, it is true to say that much more evidence exists with respect to the internal trading activities among the Yoruba towns and the trading activities of the Hausa through the Yoruba country. Richard and John Lander described a small Yoruba town (Bumbum) near Kishi (north of Oyo) as being "a lively little walled town, a great thoroughfare for *fatakies* of merchants, trading from Hausa, Borgu and other countries to Gonja [in northern Ghana]."[20]

The important point to note is the antiquity of re-

17 Jack Goody, "The Akan and the North," *Ghana Notes and Queries*, no. 9 (November 1966), 18-24.

18 Joseph Dupuis, *Journal of a Residence in Ashantee* (1824; rpt., London: Frank Cass, 1966), pp. xxviii and cviii.

19 Hugh Clapperton, *Journal of a Second Expedition into the Interior of Africa* (London: John Murray, 1829), p. 138.

20 Richard and John Lander, *Journal of an Expedition to Explore the Course and Termination of the Niger*, vol. 1 (London: John Murray, 1832), p. 153.

gional mobility of trading groups within and across West Africa. Although I have emphasized the traditional importance of a few ethnic groups, notably the Mande, the Zerma, the Hausa, and the Yoruba, in this type of mobility, a small number of members of other ethnic groups are also involved. These include traditionally the Nupes of Nigeria, the Fon of Dahomey, and the Akan of Ghana.

MOVEMENTS OF FISHERMEN AND FARMERS

Apart from the mobility of traders, there was considerable mobility of fishermen. Following various waterways, whether rivers or lagoons, in search of fertile fishing grounds, this type of people has often had to settle in territories of other ethnic groups and has thereby stimulated intercourse between these areas and their home region. The mobility of two of these fishing groups will be described to give some idea of their range of movements. The first group comprises the Sorkawa who are believed to have derived originally from the Sorko of Songhai.[21] Their main base is in the Kebbi district of Sokoto Province of Nigeria at the confluence of the Sokoto and Niger rivers (fig. 7). Their colonies are to be found all along the rivers Sokoto, Niger, and Benue from Timbuktu in the west to Aboh at the mouth of the delta. Although principally Muslim, the Sorkawa fishermen have been able to live among numerous non-Muslim ethnic groups. The Sorkawa regard themselves as having descended from Faran Maka Boté who is the founder of the Songhai ruling family in Gao. Although P. G. Harris would put the date much earlier, Rouch suggests that they were probably established at their

21 See P. G. Harris, "The Kebbi Fishermen (Sokoto Province, Nigeria)," *Journal of the Royal Anthropological Institute*, 72, pts. 1 and 2 (1942): 23-32, and Harris, "Notes on Yauri (Sokoto Province, Nigeria)," *Journal of the Royal Anthropological Institute*, 60 (1930): 283-334.

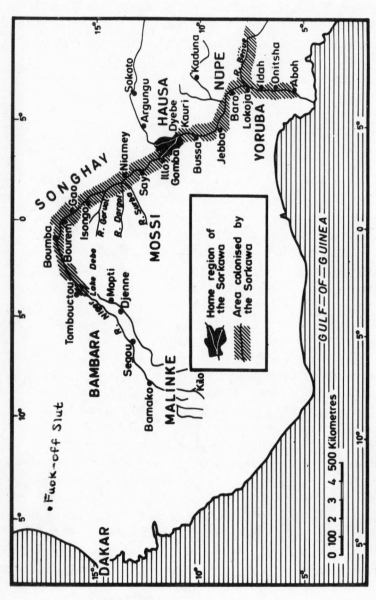

Fig. 7. Sorkawa Migration

SOURCE: Jean Rouch, "Les Sorkawa, pêcheurs itinérants du moyen Niger," *Africa*, 20, no. 1 (January 1950): 6.

present base from about the sixteenth century following the Moroccan invasion of Songhai.[22] How far they had spread before the colonial period is difficult to say. Rouch again suggests that it was about 1920 that they reached Niamey and that they got to Timbuktu only in 1949. To the south, too, he suspects that it was only with the establishment of the *pax Britannica* that they gained access throughout the Nupe country where there existed a well-organized guild of fishermen.

The second group of migrating fishermen is the Anlo branch of the Ewe people. From their homeland in Ghana, east of the river Volta, these people are found in large or small concentrations along the West African coast from Angola in the south to Freetown (Sierra Leone) in the north.[23] Although there is no sufficient record of their movement, by the nineteenth century they were known to have been well established in Lagos, where they not only fished but performed an important role in the dangerous traffic over the surf and shoals of the entrance to the Lagos lagoon.

When we turn to the mobility of farming groups, we are faced with the difficulty of documentation. A number of reasons can explain this difficulty. This type of movement often involves a relatively small number of people, covering relatively short distances into the territory of neighbouring ethnic groups. In consequence, it often elicits little comment or notice. On the other hand, where a large number of people is involved, it takes on the character of a major colonization movement, often involving the subjugation and subservience of the

22 Jean Rouch, "Les Sorkawa, pêcheurs itinérants du moyen Niger" [The Sorkawa, Migrant Fishermen of the Middle Niger], *Africa*, 20, no. 1 (January 1950): 5-25.
23 Polly Hill, "Pan-African Fishermen," *West Africa*, no. 2430 (28 December 1963): 1455, and no. 2431 (4 January 1964): 14-15.

host community. What we are concerned with here, however, is the peaceful movement of a sufficiently large number of people from one ethnic group into the land of another for purposes of agriculture and without subjugating the host community. Emphasis on a "peaceful" incursion need not be overly stressed, since friction of one type or the other cannot be completely ruled out. Another characteristic of this type of movement is that it tends to occur among people exerting a high degree of demographic pressure on their resources and is directed into relatively empty lands owned by other ethnic groups.

West Africa provides numerous examples of ethnic groups engaged in this form of mobility. These include the Tivs and the Ibos of Nigeria, the Krobos and the Akwapims of Ghana, and the Lobis of Upper Volta. Paul Bohannan has written about the movement of the Tivs into the territory of neighbouring ethnic groups, but unfortunately his study included very little historical data about the movements.[24]

One of the best-documented movements of farming groups is that of the Krobos and Akwapims in Ghana.[25] (See fig. 8 for movement of the Krobos.) This movement is said to have dated from the early nineteenth century and involved the conscious acquisition by purchase of the land of the neighbouring Akim tribe. In its initial

[24] Paul Bohannan, "The Migration and Expansion of the Tiv," *Africa*, 24, no. 1 (January 1954): 2-16.

[25] See M. J. Field, "The Agricultural System of the Manya-Krobo of the Gold Coast," *Africa*, 14, no. 2 (April 1943): 54-65; Polly Hill, "The Migrant Cocoa Farmers of Southern Ghana," *Africa*, 31, no. 3 (July 1961): 209-30; John M. Hunter, "Cocoa Migration and Patterns of Land Ownership in the Densu Valley near Suhum, Ghana," *Transactions of the Institute of British Geographers*, 33 (December 1963): 61-88; and Marion Johnson, "Migrants' Progress," *Bulletin of the Ghana Geographical Association*, 9, no. 2 (July 1964): 4-27, and 10, no. 1 (January 1965): 13-40.

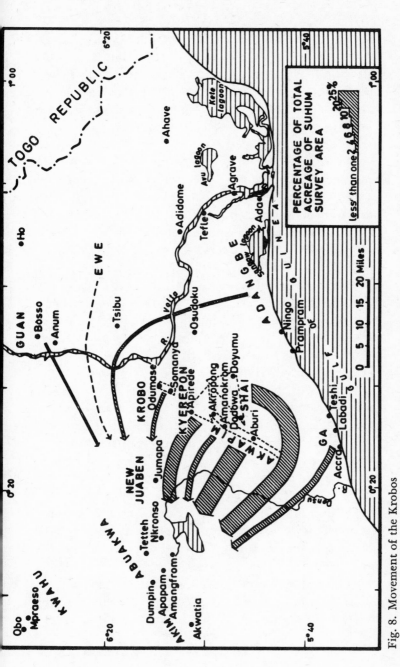

Fig. 8. Movement of the Krobos

SOURCE: John M. Hunter, "Cocoa Migration and Patterns of Land Ownership in the Densu Valley near Suhum, Ghana," *Transactions of the Institute of British Geographers*, no. 33 (December 1963): 68.

phase, the need for land among the Krobos and Akwapims was for subsistence crop production, but later cocoa cultivation became the driving force of their expansiveness. Hunter suggests that the basic method of movement was in the manner of leap-frogging. A Krobo or Akwapim farmer purchased a piece of virgin forest, commonly within a day's walk of the starting point of migration, cleared and cultivated it, and then re-invested any income accruing in the purchase of a second piece of land farther west. By this process of continuous re-investment, the farmer moved steadily westwards during the course of his lifetime, acquiring one new land after another. The similarity of this process of expansion to the opening of the American West is, no doubt, very obvious. Thanks to the advent of motor transportation in the 1920s, the distance covered in each "leap" became progressively lengthened. Today, this never-ending search for new land has taken the Krobo and Akwapim farmers as far west as the frontier with the Ivory Coast, a distance of over two hundred miles from their home base.

A feature of this leap-frogging movement is that it is always undertaken in groups. At each new location, the group establishes a new settlement usually distinct from that of their host. None of these settlements is, however, regarded as home. Each year, at the time of the annual festival of their home settlement, many of the farmers return to visit their relations and participate in the remembrance of elders who have passed away. The home settlement is also visited for the performance of traditional wedding and funeral rites, and for the settling of family disputes.

Another example of migrating farming communities is the Lobi (fig. 9). The Lobi number about one hundred and twenty thousand and live in the Gaoua district of

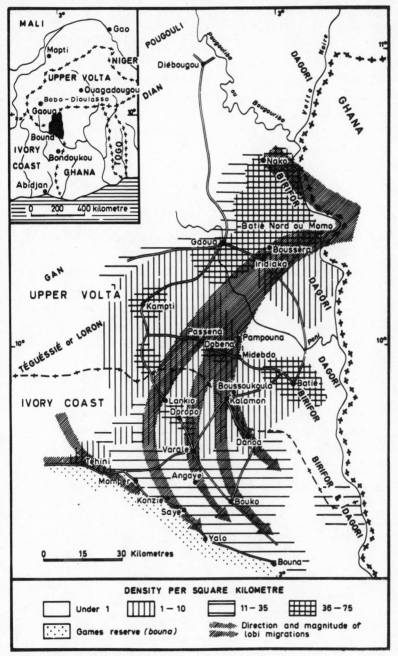

Fig. 9. Movement of the Lobi
SOURCE: Georges Savonnet, "La colonisation du pays Koulango (Haute Côte d'Ivoire) par les Lobi de Haute-Volta," *Les Cahiers d'Outre Mer*, 15, no. 57 (January-March 1962): 29.

Upper Volta, close to the Black Volta River. It is estimated that nearly one-fourth of these people have moved
out in a series of leap-frog steps into northern Ghana and
the Ivory Coast. Georges Savonnet suggests that the Lobi
originally lived east of the Black Volta River in what is
now modern Ghana, that they began to cross to the west
bank into Upper Volta at the end of the eighteenth
century, and that from here they had continued their
migration southward into the northern districts of the
Ivory Coast.[26] By the first half of the nineteenth century,
some of them had already reached Midebdo, Pampouna,
and Boussoukoula, and by the end of the century, they
were to be found at Danoa and at Varale. In the first
thirty years of this century, they had reached the vicinity
of Saye, Yalo, and Bouna further south where about
four thousand of them are to be found today. All in all,
in less than two centuries, the Lobi have traversed a
distance southward into the Ivory Coast of between 75
to 120 miles. In Ghana, their southward movement has
also been noted, especially in the Gonja region.[27] An
entry in the West Gonja District Record Book of 1919
refers to only twelve Lobi compounds in the area. By
1948, the census returns showed the population of Lobi
in the area had risen to over seven thousand.

Again, as in the initial phase of the movement of the
Krobos and Akwapims, the Lobi migrations have been
undertaken largely for the purpose of acquiring land
to grow more subsistence crops. Savonnet suggests that
a primary reason for this mobility of the Lobi is their

26 Georges Savonnet, "La colonisation du pays Koulango (Haute Côte
d'Ivoire) par les Lobi de Haute-Volta," *Les Cahiers d'Outre Mer*, 15,
no. 57 (January–March 1962): 25-46; see also Henri Labouret, *Tribus
du Rameau Lobi* [Tribes of the Lobi Branch] (Paris: Institut d'Ethnolo-
gie, 1931).
27 W. Manshard, "Land Use Patterns and Agricultural Migration in
Central Ghana (Western Gonja)," *Tijdscrift voor Economische en
Sociale Geografie*, 52, no. 9 (September 1961): 225-30.

practice of shifting cultivation which, with an increase in population above the critical level, must result in periodic migrations of the surplus population. This suggestion can hardly be valid, since the farming methods of the Lobi are not basically different from those of the less mobile community among whom they sojourn. However, Savonnet adduces other reasons to account for the mobility of the Lobi. These include religious and social factors, especially the absence in their belief system of any connection between their ancestral spirit and a particular location, as well as their extreme individualism and lack of a social organization above the level of a clan.

I believe I have said enough to indicate the complexity of traditional mobility within West Africa. I have not, however, concerned myself with two other significant movements—that of the nomadic herdsmen and that of the missionaries. Derrick Stenning called attention to the intricate pattern of nomadic mobility which has carried the Fulani from west to east for over eight centuries across the whole of the grassland area of West Africa.[28] Similarly, there are studies which show that, apart from the early proselytizing activities of Muslim preachers and the nineteenth-century efforts of European Christian missionaries, new syncretist groups in West Africa engage in movements which take them far away from their home base. A good example is provided by the story of the Aladura sect, otherwise known as the Church of the Lord.[29] Begun in 1930 by a Yoruba of Western Nigeria origin, leaders of this sect moved to

[28] Derrick J. Stenning, "Transhumance, Migratory Drift, Migration: Patterns of Pastoral Fulani Nomadism," *Journal of the Royal Anthropological Institute*, 87, pt. 1 (1957): 57-74.

[29] H. W. Turner, "The Church of the Lord: The Expansion of a Nigerian Independent Church in Sierra Leone and Ghana," *Journal of African History*, 3, no. 1 (1962): 91-110.

Lagos in 1943, to Sierra Leone and Liberia in 1947, and then to Ghana in 1953. In all these places, the church grew in size and number by attracting not only local Yoruba but an increasingly large number of the indigenous people.

TRADITIONAL RECEPTION ARRANGEMENTS FOR MIGRANTS

The important point to emphasize is that mobility of a completely different type from the colonial labour migration had been going on in West Africa long before the colonial period. This traditional mobility had developed its own norms and practices, many of which came to be eroded during the colonial period. The most important of these norms was that the stranger community accepted the idea that they were under the control of the local political authorities and that its members could stay in the area only on the sufferance of their hosts. Detailed arrangements were made to ensure that friction between the two communities was kept to a minimum and also that the stranger community, as soon as it was large enough, enjoyed a high degree of internal autonomy.

In the urban areas, the arrangements took one of two forms. Especially where the number of strangers was not very large, the local ruler appointed one of his chiefs to take charge of matters affecting the strangers. Alternatively, where the strangers formed a sizeable community, they were encouraged to live in separate wards, sometimes called *zongos,* under the control of their own chief or headman. Here, they would practise their own religion and socially organize themselves as they thought fit. Their chief or headman was held responsible for the good behaviour of members of his community, especially in their dealings with members of the host community. He was summoned periodically to the court of the local ruler to be apprised of any developments in the town which might affect his people. In some areas, the headman of the strangers had no direct access to the local ruler, but dealt with him through the intermediary of a chief in charge of strangers.

The historical origins of this practice are not easy to trace. Es Sadi described Timbuktu about 1352, the time of the visit of Ibn Battuta, as being "inhabited mostly by people of Mimah and by Tawarek [Molathemin], especially Masufa, who had a headman of their own, while the Melle governor [of the city] was Farba Musa."[30] Much later, in 1819, Dupuis described a similar practice in Kumasi where Muslim traders from the north were to be found. He reported a conversation with the headman of the stranger community which is worth quoting as it throws some light on the points that have been made. Says the headman: "My avocations at Coomassy are several; but my chief employment is a school which I have endowed, and which I preside over myself. . . . Besides this, the king's heart is turned towards me, and I am a favoured servant. Over the Moslems I rule as Cady, conformably to our law; I am also a member of the king's council in affairs relating to the believers of Sarem and Dagomba; and I trade with foreign countries through the agency of my friend Abou Beer."[31] S. F. Nadel also mentioned that at Bida, capital of the Nupe country, traders from the north and south, individual traders, and the strangers who settle down for longer periods, perhaps permanently, live in a section of the town called *làlemi,* under their own headmen.[32]

It is possible to multiply examples of similar practices

30 See Heinrich Barth, *Travels and Discoveries in North and Central Africa,* vol. 3 (1857–59; rpt., London: Frank Cass, 1965), p. 663.

31 Dupuis, p. 97.

32 S. F. Nadel, *A Black Byzantium* (London: Oxford University Press, 1942), p. 120.

dating from pre-colonial times in cities in various other parts of West Africa. But the widely scattered nature of the few examples chosen would attest to the almost universal nature of the practice. In the rural areas, the position is slightly different, since the stranger community does not have to live physically close to its host. Indeed, most stranger communities prefer to stay well away from the host village. However, periodical gifts or tribute to the host chief are expected to underline the dependent status of the stranger community. Savonnet reports, for instance, that the Lobi have to present to the host chief of Koulango a cow and 10,000 cowries at the time of settlement and, in addition, one or more chickens, quantities of shea-butter, millet, and guinea corn each year.[33] Similarly, gifts to the head of the host community are expected when the land being used is held under a system of tenancy. In Ghana, such gifts are known as *abusa*, literally meaning one-third of the yield of the farm. Among the Yoruba, it is known as the *isha-kole*. However, it would appear that in cases such as those of the Krobos and Akwapims where the outright sale of land to the stranger community is involved, no such reminder of a dependent status is entertained. Even in this case, the stranger community tries scrupulously to prevent any type of friction with their host.

IMPACT OF THE COLONIAL REGIME

The colonial period clearly brought about tremendous changes in the pattern and magnitude of regional mobility in West Africa. In the first place, it considerably increased the number of people involved in these movements. It is suggested that in most years probably between two and three million people are involved in movements out of their home areas. Secondly, the colon-

[33] Savonnet, p. 41.

ial period saw the imposition on the traditional criss-cross pattern of movements of a stronger north-south or interior-to-coast orientation largely of seasonal or short-term agricultural labour. Thirdly, transportation development during the colonial period lengthened the distances which migrants could traverse, whilst improvement in communications widened the knowledge of the existence and distribution of employment opportunities. Fourthly, by its very nature, the colonial administration destroyed or weakened the immediacy of the relation between the migrants and their host community. Even in the British colonies where the indirect rule system operated, the strangers came to look for protection ultimately from the colonial administrator and not from the local ruler. Indeed, the Emir of Kano was reported to have written a letter to the British Resident early in the 1930s in which he asked "how men could come and reside at the gates of the city and have dealings with men of the city and yet not be subject to the rules of the city."[34] He also pointed out that some of his subjects who chose to live among the strangers may come to claim that, like the strangers, they were no longer under his authority and that their insubordination may constitute a serious threat to the stability of his administration.

This protest, in fact, is one illustration of the undermining of local traditional authority and its replacement by colonial administrative and judicial practices which were less discriminatory between migrants and their host community. To the extent that the British Resident or the French *Commandant de Cercle* became the penultimate arbiter in the relation within and between each of the two groups, it can be said that the existence of strangers' quarters in most cities no longer had any

[34] Margery Perham, *Native Administration in Nigeria* (London: Oxford University Press, 1937), p. 101.

77

political or judicial significance, but was simply a matter of social differentiation. Indeed, in the case of the French West African colonies, the obliteration of the distinction between the two groups in terms of their position before the law was completed by a decree of 1946 which "abolished native penal law and placed all inhabitants [of the colonies] under the jurisdiction of the French Code and French penal laws."[35] Even in the British colonial territories where the operation of the indirect rule may give a contrary impression, James Coleman rightly observed that "the native administrations were in effect but local extensions of the British superstructure. Although the British paid no little attention to matters of form and ceremony, everybody knew where real power was vested."[36]

In short, by establishing a fairly uniform system of administration and justice over the whole territory, the colonial administration in West Africa considerably enhanced the status of migrants within the community in which they lived. When on top of this, towards the end of the regime, it introduced notions of representative and democratically elected local administration, the position of the migrant was finally transformed. His dependent status was terminated and he could now compete with his erstwhile host for political power. Where the host community was outnumbered and economically outpaced by the strangers, a situation of considerable anxiety and bitterness was created.

One final consequence of the colonial regime on regional mobility was that the regional mobility came to involve a larger number of ethnic groups, most of whom had not been important in the pre-colonial movements.

35 Robert Delavignette, *Freedom and Authority in French West Africa* (London: Oxford University Press, 1950), p. 85.
36 James S. Coleman, *Nigeria: Background to Nationalism* (Berkeley: University of California Press, 1958), p. 54.

The implication of this was that members of such ethnic groups were largely oblivious of the traditional norms and practices in these matters and never seriously developed any immediate relationship with their host community.

Perhaps the best example of such an ethnic group is the Ibo of Nigeria. Before the colonial period, very few Ibos were to be found outside their home area east and west of the lower Niger River. Their dispersion from this base to all parts of Nigeria is closely related to the expansion of the railway from Port Harcourt in the Niger Delta through the Ibo country to link up with the Lagos-Kano line in 1927. Their arrival in significant number was noted at most of the main centres along the rail line. But nowhere is this fact as well documented as in Lagos where the Ibo began to be found in large numbers only after 1931 when the railway bridge over the river Benue had been completed and the direct route from Port Harcourt through Kaduna to Lagos had been established.[37] The 1911 census of Lagos recorded only 264 Ibos in a population of 74,000. By 1921, their number had risen to 1,609, and had jumped to over 5,000 by 1931. The 1950 census recorded 25,600 Ibos, and the indications were that by 1963, there were over 70,000 Ibos in Lagos. Their number were also considerable in most of the major cities like Ibadan, Kano, Zaria, Kaduna, and Jos. Apart from those in the urban areas, a sizeable number had moved into the rural areas of the less numerous Ibibio and Igalla peoples where they worked as migrant tenant farmers.[38] Further afield in various parts of Western Nigeria, Ibos also provided vitally needed hired labour, especially for the harvesting of the oil palm.

[37] Mabogunje, *Urbanization in Nigeria*, p. 264.
[38] R. K. Udo, "The Migrant Tenant Farmers in Eastern Nigeria," *Africa*, 34, no. 4 (October 1964): 326-39.

The point to stress is the lack of any immediate relationship — based on tradition — between the stranger and the host community for those groups that became involved in extensive regional mobility during the colonial period. Even in the case of groups with a longer tradition of such movements, the weakening of the relation between the host and stranger community during the colonial period is evident. An understanding of the effect of this situation becomes very important in any attempt at evaluating the trend and prospects of regional mobility in West Africa.

Conclusion

Let me conclude by relating what I have said so far to the conceptual framework which I set out in my previous chapter. The situation in most of West Africa up to the end of the colonial era can be described as pre-national and pre-industrial. Regional mobility went on extensively in West Africa involving people of different ethnic groups. Before the colonial era, assimilation of the migrants was not easy or even desired, given the pre-industrial nature of the economy. But fairly widespread institutional arrangements were made to accommodate the migrants as part of the local community. This allowed relatively intimate, though circumscribed, interaction to take place between the local and the migrant communities. The imposition of the colonial administration weakened or rendered unnecessary the continuance of these age-old institutional arrangements and contributed immensely to some of the uncertainties and difficulties faced by migrants as West Africa after 1957 moved into what I have called the national, pre-industrial phase of its history. I shall return to this theme more fully in my final chapter.

CHAPTER III:
EFFECTS OF REGIONAL MOBILITY
ON RESOURCE DEVELOPMENT

REGIONAL MOBILITY has been defined as the movement of individuals or groups of individuals across ethnic or national boundaries. Implicit in this definition is the idea that these migrants are people not only seeking new opportunities in the environment but also transmitting cultural objects, values, or traits, some of which become crucial for their effort at resource development. The important distinction here is that unlike the more recent colonial labour movement, these migrants contribute more than their physical labour to the development of resources. Their major role is often as innovators in terms of either institutions, techniques, values, or actual physical objects created or introduced into the environment.

I do not intend to underestimate the tremendous contribution of the purely colonial labour movement to resource development in West Africa, especially in respect of export agricultural production. Indeed, it is a well-known fact that in many of the West African countries, the contribution of agriculture to the export trade would fall drastically if all migrant labour were to be withdrawn. In Gambia, for example, it is estimated that one-third of the annual tonnage of the groundnut export is due to the activities of the stranger farmers. According to Reginald Jarrett, these stranger farmers arrive in the Gambia between March and June each year, grow their crops on land for which the resident landlord receives two or three days' labour per week, and depart back to the interior in December.[1] Both the landlord farmers and the trading firms consider the immigrant farmers an asset to the economy, despite the increased burden they put on local food supplies. And, to offset this liability, the stranger farmers are even required to add the growing of food crops, especially grains, to their primary function. In Ghana, to take another example, Jean Rouch estimated that between 1953 and 1955 migrant labour from French West African territories accounted for some 40 per cent of the manual labour force and in most years brought about £6 million into the French territories.[2] Moreover, he pointed out that nearly 75 per cent of agricultural workers on cocoa farms in Ghana are immigrants of one sort or the other. Immigrants also make up 55 per cent of mine workers, 37 per cent of timber workers, 22 per cent of industrial workers, 36 per cent of labourers engaged in public works in Accra, and 16 per cent of clerical staff in commercial houses.[3] The same story can be told for other coastal West African countries such as Senegal, Sierra Leone, and the Ivory Coast. In Nigeria, migrants have also been of crucial importance in the export production of cocoa, palm oil, rubber, and timber as well as in mining operations. Most of the migrants in this case, however, are people from other parts of the country.

It is therefore clear that in terms of the movement of labour, regional mobility of the purely colonial type has

[1] H. Reginald Jarrett, "The Strange Farmers of the Gambia," *Geographical Review*, 39, no. 4 (October 1949): 649-57.

[2] Jean Rouch, "Migrations au Ghana (Enquête 1953–55)," *Journal de la Société des Africanistes*, 26, fasc. 1 and 2 (1956): 33-196. For an abridged English translation of this article, see "Migrations from French Territories into Ghana — Field Studies," *Africa*, 28, no. 2 (April 1958): 156-59.

[3] Rouch, "Migrations au Ghana," pp. 101-103.

been a decisive factor in resource development. What is not so clear is the importance of the other type of migrant who is not in search of wage employment but who, through his enterprise, his economic foresight, and his eagerness to innovate, has brought about significant resource development in different parts of West Africa. It is this category of migrants that we will focus upon.

It is possible to discuss the contributions of this type of migrant under four headings: institutions, techniques, objects, and values. Each contribution will be regarded as an element or a factor in resource development, if it helps to stimulate or sustain activities concerned with widening the demand for or supply of particular goods or services. In other words, such a contribution is not seen as a directly productive factor, but if its absence reduces the scope of productive activities or makes it difficult to sustain such activities over a relatively long period of time, it is regarded as significant for resource development.

DEVELOPMENT OF INSTITUTIONS

Ethnic Associations

The most important of those contributions of an institutional nature which have been due to regional mobility and which have had real importance for resource development are ethnic unions or the *associations d'originaire* of the French. These are voluntary associations of people from the same home town or home area in distant lands. It is significant that such unions are seldom found in the home area, except as deriving from the activities of the numerous units set up in distant places. In other words, the institution of unions is a direct response to movement away from the home base, a response necessitated by the need to survive in a foreign territory, an innovative activity based on a qualitative reorganization of traditional norms and resulting in part from a deprivation of essentials.

The existence of ethnic unions thus raises two crucial questions for any appreciation of the relation of regional mobility to resource development. What needs do these unions serve, and to what extent are these needs related to resource development? The best known study on ethnic unions in West Africa has been done by Kenneth Little.[4] According to Little, ethnic unions or associations have arisen in general out of the need to adapt traditional institutions to urban conditions of life and labour. He, of course, does not suggest that such associations are traditional, but he does point out that they have grown out of a prominent and accustomed feature of traditional life, that of association on lines other than kinship. Outside the ethnic area, their role partly subsumes that of kinship relation. Although Little emphasizes the urban significance of these associations, there is need to distinguish between the fact of their primarily urban location and the spread of their membership to rural migrants.

The primary social purpose of the ethnic associations is to facilitate the reception and integration of a new immigrant into the local community into which he has moved. This involves a responsibility to house the immigrant in the first few days or weeks after his arrival and to help him seek employment or settle him in a job. With respect to housing, some associations, notably that of the Yoruba in Kumasi, run what is more or less a hostel for immigrants, although the more usual practice is for the

[4] Kenneth Little, *West African Urbanization: A Study of Voluntary Associations in Social Change* (Cambridge: At the University Press, 1965). See also Little, "The Urban Role of Tribal Associations in West Africa," *African Studies*, 21, no. 1 (1962): 1-9, and Little, "The Organization of Voluntary Associations in West Africa," *Civilisations*, 9, no. 3 (1959): 283-300.

newcomer to lodge with a "countryman" or "townsman." Another social purpose served by the associations is that of fostering loyalty to and keeping migrants in touch with events in their home area. This they do through weekly, fortnightly, or monthly meetings and through encouraging participation in various social occasions connected with events in the life of individual members. The associations also serve as a form of insurance or mutual aid agency. Members are helped to meet burdensome expenses, such as those incurred by getting married, by sickness, or by the death of a near relative. In some cases, ethnic associations have sponsored the establishment of mosques, churches, and schools to cater to the needs of their members and those of the host community where the latter is favourably disposed to such gestures. Many associations have tried to regulate interpersonal relations among their members and between them and members of the host community. In this connection, the tacit role of Justice of the Peace conferred on the headman or chief of various immigrant communities by the local ruler or the colonial administration is of crucial importance. Whilst the practice is for small subdivisions of individual ethnic groups to try to regulate the affairs of their members, only those issues which they fail to settle to the satisfaction of all concerned are then appealed to the headman.[5]

It may be argued that very few of the social functions of ethnic associations have any significance for resource development. While this may be true in a general sense, their importance can be demonstrated in detail on two

[5] There are many similarities between the functions of ethnic associations in West Africa and those of various minority groups, such as the Jews in Britain. See Maurice Friedman, ed., *A Minority in Britain: Social Studies of the Anglo-Jewish Community* (London: Valentine Mitchell, 1955), and Fuad I. Khuri, "Kinship, Emigration and Trade Partnership among the Lebanese of West Africa," *Africa*, 35, no. 4 (October 1965): 385-95.

specific grounds. By absorbing the burden of the reception and integration of immigrants, the associations make the host community less sensitive to the presence of the strangers in their midst. Also, by striving to reduce the area of friction among immigrants and between them and members of the host community, they facilitate the social acceptability of the immigrants. On this latter point, Gloria Marshall notes that for the Yoruba in Kumasi this function of the ethnic associations is regarded as not without its economic benefits. For, by keeping matters out of the courts, members are saved the costs of lawyers and are spared court fees and fines.[6] At any rate, it is clear that although the social functions of ethnic associations do not of themselves stimulate resource development, they do help to sustain such effort by ensuring that disruptive incidents are kept to a minimum.

Ethnic associations, however, do have more direct economic impact on resource development. It has already been mentioned that the associations try to help new immigrants to get employment or to settle down in their trades. In this latter respect, they have been known to provide much needed initial capital for such members. They have also been known to offer loans to those members whose businesses falter. Their role in this connection can be very vital when one remembers the near impossibility of getting the foreign-owned banks to offer credit facilities to small African enterprises. Indeed, as Oyeaka Offodile quite rightly claimed, the economic function of ethnic associations as possible suppliers of credit was the inspiration behind the formation in Nigeria of what are today perhaps the most successful indigenous African banks, the African Continental and the National Banks.[7]

[6] Gloria Marshall, "Yorubas in Ghana: Report on Research Progress" (unpublished paper, University of Ibadan, 1968).
[7] E. P. Oyeaka Offodile, "Growth and Influence of Tribal Unions," *West African Review*, 18, no. 239 (August 1947): 937-41.

The most significant sphere of direct economic activity by ethnic associations is with respect to their home area. It is for this reason that there are subdivisions of the larger ethnic associations, each subdivision being identified with specific towns or clan areas. It is also for this reason that these subdivisions, apart from being a unit of the overall ethnic association in a foreign country, serve simultaneously as a branch of an improvement league, progressive union, or development society of their particular town or clan. Thus, for instance, the Shaki Parapo (or the association of people from Shaki, a town in Western Nigeria) in Kumasi, Ghana, is a unit of the Yoruba community in Kumasi. But it is also the Kumasi branch of the world-wide Shaki Improvement League. In this latter capacity, the Shaki Parapo deliberates on many matters concerned with investments and development back in Shaki. Such branches have been known to contribute substantially to the cost of building schools, mosques, churches, town halls, and post offices in their home towns. More recently, they have also subscribed to the matching grant required from local communities by the central governments for the installation of such utilities as piped water supply and electricity.

I do not intend to further belabour the significance of the institution of ethnic associations for resource development. I would argue, however, that relatively little attention has been paid, even by Kenneth Little, to their important role in this regard. Ethnic associations are clearly a response to social and economic needs demanded by regional mobility and as long as they served these needs they have been eminently successful.

The Landlord System

Another equally important institution arising from regional mobility and significant for resource development is the "landlord" institution. Polly Hill described

87

it as one in which "a 'settled stranger' makes it his business to accommodate long-distance stranger-traders and to assist them in selling, and usually in storing their goods."[8] A landlord, however, need not have been a stranger himself but, as a native, his business would be to receive long-distance traders whether native or stranger. The landlord institution has been noticed most among Hausas, especially in the cattle and kola trade between the savanna and forest belts of West Africa, but there is increasing evidence that it is not peculiar to them. All the same, the Hausa version of the institution indicates its general characteristics.

Abner Cohen provides us with a good description of this institution in the cattle market at Ibadan. He emphasizes that although the word "landlord" may be regarded as the literal English translation of the Hausa *mai gida*, the latter performs several other functions in the cattle trade not usually associated with the economic or social roles of the English institution of a landlord system.[9] In the first place, the *mai gida* is a house owner having usually two houses, one of which serves as his own residence whilst the other is reserved for his dealers from the north. Sometimes, he may have a third for housing his servants, assistants, clerks, and *malams* free of charge. Cohen noted that of the twelve cattle landlords in the *Zango* at Ibadan in 1963, one had six houses, a second had four, two others had two each, and the rest had one each. Secondly, the *mai gida* serves as a middleman between his dealers and local buyers in the market. In discharging this particular duty, he engages a number of assistants who operate in the market under his direct

8 Polly Hill, "Landlords and Brokers: A West African Trading System (with a Note on Kumasi Butchers)," *Cahiers d'Etudes Africaines*, 6, no. 23 (1966): 350.

9 Abner Cohen, "The Social Organization of Credit in a West African Cattle Market," *Africa*, 35, no. 1 (January 1965): 8-20.

supervision. Thirdly, he often operates as an insurer or risk-taker. This role is of great importance, since the whole operation of the market is based largely on credit. His main function here is to guarantee that the buyer will eventually pay the agreed price. This guarantee carries the implication that if the buyer should default he would pay the full amount to the dealer himself. Such risk-taking is, of course, based on close and intimate knowledge of the credit-worthiness of potential buyers as well as long experience in the business.

To these fundamental roles of the landlord, Polly Hill, from her experience in Ghana, adds two others. She indicates that in recent times many landlords have had to serve as travel agents for their dealers, providing them with a wide range of information on such things as exchange control and import licensing. She also points out that landlords are increasingly being called upon to provide necessary storage facilities for most of their long-distance dealers who cannot hope to dispose of most of their goods during the brief six- to eight-hour period of a market day.

The question has often been asked as to what returns accrue to a landlord for his rather impressive list of investments in respect to stranger dealers. The evidence to date is that the returns are of a rather diffuse nature involving commissions on sales and brokerage charges as well as gifts. But there is no doubt that taken together they do provide for the landlord returns commensurate with this effort.

Evidence of the operation of the landlord system from other parts of West Africa can also be cited. Clapperton remarked briefly on the practice as he observed it at Koolfu in the Nupe country in 1829. "The Bornou merchants," he narrated, "during their stay, stop in the town in the houses of their friends or acquaintances, and give them a small present on their arrival and departure, for the use of the house."[10] Felix Dubois, writing in 1897 about Timbuktu, pointed out that the inhabitants are mainly brokers, contractors, and landlords. As landlords, they offer "gratuitous board and lodging to the stranger-merchant for the first three days and interpret the noble precept in a disinterested and elevated manner."[11] The part of landlord or *diatigui* does not end there. He is expected to help the trader make his purchases and to keep him fully informed on the supply of goods in the market, the current prices, and the creditworthiness of his potential buyers — all of this at no extra charge to the trader. Dorjahn and Fyfe also made numerous references to the institution, especially among trading Mandingoes and Fulanis, dating still further back to the eighteenth century.[12] They showed that this practice was sufficiently time-honoured so that there was no difficulty in extending it to the early European traders. One of these, John Matthews, described how

> when the adventurer arrives upon the coast with a suitable cargo . . . he dispatches his boats properly equipped to the different rivers. On their arrival at the place of trade they immediately apply to the headman of the town, inform him of their business, and request his protection; desiring he will either be himself their landlord, or appoint a respectable person, who becomes security for the person and goods of the stranger, and also for the recovery of all money lent, provided it is done with his knowledge and approbation. This business finished, and

10 Hugh Clapperton, *Journal of a Second Expedition into the Interior of Africa* (London: John Murray, 1829), pp. 137-38.

11 Felix Dubois, *Timbuctoo the Mysterious*, trans. Diana White (London: William Heinemann, 1897), pp. 259-60.

12 V. R. Dorjahn and Christopher Fyfe, "Landlord and Stranger: Change in Tenancy Relations in Sierra Leone," *Journal of African History*, 3, no. 3 (1962): 391-97.

proper presents made (for nothing is done without) they proceed to trade either by lending their goods to the natives, who carry them up into the country, or by waiting till trade is brought to them.[13]

The institution of landlord has, in recent times, been extended to cover the case of migrant agricultural tenants. Such stranger farmers, especially if they are young and unmarried, regard the landlord as a patron and something of a "father figure." Dorjahn and Fyfe point out that among the Temne such a landlord is expected to help his unmarried tenant "in amassing the bride-wealth necessary for marriage," to offer advice, and to mediate "in the event of a minor dispute."[14] Under Mende and Temne law, the landlord is held responsible for the social behaviour of his tenant and has the duty of pleading the tenant's cause in the court of the Paramount in the event that he offends local custom or usage. He may also have to help him pay his tax or provide food or seed rice to tide over a bad year. In return for all this, the stranger tenant may give his landlord each year a share of his harvest, help to "brush" his farms, and refrain from surreptitiously harvesting oil palms and certain fruit trees on the land assigned to him. He may also become very attached to his landlord's household, bringing occasional small gifts and spreading the fact of his landlord's generosity.

Enough has been said to show how this institution, itself a product of regional mobility, has been crucial in stimulating resource development. Although at a rather unsophisticated level, the institution serves the same purpose as a modern bank in facilitating exchange through the extension of credit, as a modern insurance house, and as a trade information bureau. That it still

13 John Matthews, *A Voyage to the River Sierra-Leone* (1788; rpt. London: Frank Cass, 1966), pp. 142-43.
14 Dorjahn and Fyfe, p. 392.

continues to flourish is testimony to the great needs which it continues to serve. And until the scale of business organization in West Africa changes radically, it is unlikely that this institution will lose its importance or significance.

Diffusion of Techniques

A wide variety of techniques have been transferred by immigrant groups into new areas and have helped to stimulate the production of new commodities or to increase the supply of existing ones. A few examples of such transfer of techniques will suffice.

The first example illustrates a change in fishing techniques used by the inhabitants along the Kebbi River in the Sokoto Province of Nigeria. The people of this riverain area are known as the Kebbawa, and although they have always been noted for their fishing activities, their techniques have been restricted largely to trapping the fish. For this purpose, they have evolved a wide variety of hand-nets and traps, some of which are masterpieces of ingenuity. In spite of this equipment, it was clear that they were far from fully exploiting the fish resources of the rivers. In the sixteenth century there arrived the migrant group of fishermen, the Sorkawa, and from them the local inhabitants learnt what is today their most important technique of fishing — the *taru* technique. "The *taru* itself is a large seine of dimensions roughly 30 feet by 60 feet. Both top and bottom of the net have rope extensions (*shembi*) for holding and for pulling in the net. The top end of the net has floats of bamboo palm (*karu*), while the bottom end is weighted with stones."[15] P. G. Harris describes in detail the actual method of fishing with a *taru*. According to him, the *taru*

15 P. G. Harris, "The Kebbi Fishermen (Sokoto Province, Nigeria)," *Journal of the Royal Anthropological Institute*, 72, pts. 1 and 2 (1942): 26.

party consists of three boats and five persons. The first boat is occupied by one person called the beater whose task it is to beat the water and frighten the fish into the net; the other two boats are each occupied by one fisherman and his paddler holding a half part of the net. The introduction of this technique occasioned something of a revolution in the fishing industry on the Kebbi River. And to that extent, it underlines the type of innovative activity that often results from unimpeded regional mobility.

Agriculture also provides us with other examples of innovative activities resulting from regional mobility in West Africa. Perhaps the best documented of these is the technique of land purchase and land division evolved by migrating Krobo farmers and disseminated over much of southern Ghana. There is no evidence that this method was traditional in the home areas of the Krobo, but no sooner had they begun their migratory expansion than they evolved the system of land acquisition which is now popularly known as the *huza* system.

Detailed description of the *huza* system is provided in the studies by Field, Hunter, and Hill;[16] it is enough in this chapter simply to outline the broad features of the system and to evaluate its significance for resource development. The word *huza* refers to a piece of land bought by a group of people who may or may not be kinsmen, but who act for the purpose under a leader. This leader is often elected and comes to be regarded as the father of the *huza*. It is he who enters into and concludes negotiations with the seller. This corporate character of the *huza* ends with the purchase and does not extend to the actual ownership of the land. As such, the use of the word "company" as the English equivalent of a *huza* can lead to confusion. Once the land is bought, it is immedi-

16 See chap. 2, n. 25.

ately shared out among members of the *huza,* each receiving the equivalent of his subscription. His ownership right is absolute and includes the right to alienate or sell the land if he so desires. In other words, "As a corporate body, then, the company is purely transitory: it comes into being to arrange the purchase and subsequent division of land, and it is dissolved as soon as this is achieved. It was, and remains today, the stranger-farmers' collective bargaining device."[17]

The system works somewhat as follows. The leader, once he has been elected, travels west (perhaps accompanied by a few members of the company) to meet an Akim Chief who is known to have land for sale. He inspects this land and makes a personal estimate of its worth, bearing in mind its size, soil fertility, proportion of swamp area, rock outcrop, and over-steep slopes. Bargaining then takes place and a price is agreed upon. At this stage, the area of land is not known, only its boundaries. If the leader is wealthy, he may purchase the land outright or, alternatively, secure it on a deposit collected from the company members. These members do not figure in the purchase of the land. They are represented by the leader who deals personally with the vendor chief.

When the land is bought and all members of the company have been assembled, an ingenious system of land subdivision is now engaged upon (fig. 10). A straight line, known as a baseline, is cut through the property near the boundary and its length is measured. The unit of measurement is the *kpa* or rope which in turn is based on the indigenous unit of length, the *gugwe.* The *gugwe* is the length which a tall man can compass when he stretches his arms sideways and is roughly equivalent to an English fathom or six feet. Usually, the rope is seven

17 John M. Hunter, "Cocoa Migration and Patterns of Land Ownership in the Densu Valley near Suhum, Ghana," *Transactions of the Institute of British Geographers,* 33 (December 1963): 74-75.

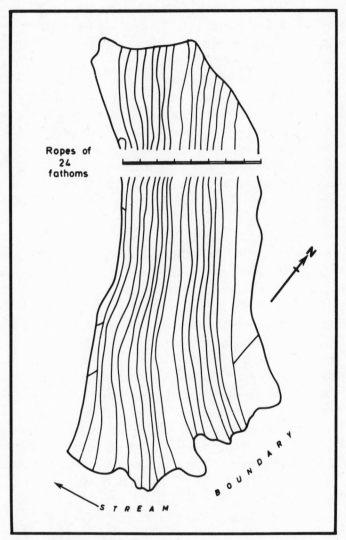

Ropes of
24
fathoms

STREAM

BOUNDARY

Fig. 10. *Huza* Land Division

SOURCE: John M. Hunter, "Cocoa Migration and Patterns of Land Ownership in the Densu Valley near Suhum, Ghana," *Transactions of the Institute of British Geographers*, no. 33 (December 1963): 79.

gugwi (about fourteen yards), but it may be five or twelve *gugwi*. Indeed, the length of a rope varies from company to company and is often a matter of agreement among members of the company.[18]

Once the length of the baseline is known, the share-out among the company members can proceed. Each member takes land in proportion to his contribution to the cost of the land. At any rate, demand is always arranged to equate with supply. Occasionally, a farmer may withdraw his deposit if he is not satisfied with the proposed share-out. A small *huza* may be parcelled out among fifty to sixty members and a large one to as many as three hundred members.

Further subdivisions of *huzas* have gone on with each passing generation. As is the custom in many patrilineal societies, the land of a farmer passes on his death to his sons. These sons, in turn, subdivide the land longitudinally so that the strips become narrower and narrower. Their land, however, is not shared equally among sons, but according to the number of wives. This means that where one of a man's wives has many sons, each of these would tend to receive a much smaller share of the strip.

Most of the writers on this interesting custom of the Krobos have tried to link it closely with the fact that the Krobos are basically a patrilineal society. They have tried to draw validity for this point of view by contrasting the *huza* system with the "family" system of land purchase and land division found among the neighbouring migratory, but matrilineal, Akropong. It is difficult to see what prevents a matrilineal society from accepting or adopting the *huza* system, since it is largely at the point of inheritance that the major differences between the two lineage systems show, not at the point at which

18 M. J. Field, "The Agricultural System of the Manya-Krobo of the Gold Coast," *Africa*, 14, no. 2 (April 1943): 55.

a farmer is acquiring the land for himself. Furthermore, very few of these migratory farmers are restricted to land-holding on a single *huza*. The more general practice is for a farmer to own land on numerous *huzas* spread across southern Ghana from east to west.

It is now possible to evaluate this technique of land acquisition in terms of its significance for resource development. It is a well-known fact that in the history of agricultural development, increasing individualization of landholding is an important prerequisite for significant commercialization of agriculture. In Great Britain in the period up to the eighteenth century, this type of movement towards individualization of farm holdings (which became known as the Enclosure Movement) was an important prelude to significant changes and development in British agriculture. In Africa today, individualization of holdings is also being canvassed as a major prerequisite for rapid agricultural development. The activities of the government of Kenya are perhaps best known in this respect. One reason for this correlation between individualization of holdings and commercialization of agriculture is that freehold ownership of land is a first step towards making land a negotiable asset that can be leased out, mortgaged, or sold outright to raise funds for improvement or for other types of investment activities. To the extent that the *huza* system contributes to releasing land from the trammels of traditional conception of ownership, it can be shown to have had great significance for resource development in Ghana.

Indeed, Polly Hill emphasizes that the migratory expansion of the Krobo can be fully appreciated only within the framework of rural capitalism at work. According to her, "the essential nature of the migratory process is that it is forward-looking, prospective, provident, prudential — the opposite of hand-to-mouth. Had

97

the farmers, like so many retail traders, simply been concerned to 'get rich quick' and then go out of business, they would, to use their own terminology, have 'eaten' the proceeds from their early cocoa farms, rather than re-investing them in other lands. . . . Almost from the beginning, cocoa farms established on purchased land were regarded as investments — i.e. property which existed for the purpose of giving rise to further property." It must be admitted it is almost impossible to estimate the actual contribution of the migrant farmers to cocoa production, even approximately. However, on the basis of shipments from the railway station at Pakro, an important centre on the route between Akwapim and Akim Abuakwa, Hill suggests that in the 1920s and 1930s perhaps about two-thirds of the one hundred thousand tons or more cocoa produced in the Eastern Provinces came from the migrants' farms. But there is no basis for making a similar estimate of the contribution of the migrants to cocoa production in the Western Provinces.[19]

Apart from land, the migrant farmers also engaged in other forms of productive investments. These included house-building in their home towns, educational expenditure on their children, the building of houses for letting in such major urban centres as Accra, Kumasi, and Koforidua, the buying of cocoa and other produce (no longer of much importance), and lorry ownership and operation.

One final technique to call attention to is the "rotating credit association." This is a device for encouraging capital formation and for extending credit facilities to individual members of a group of subscribers. William R. Bascom provides a detailed description of this technique, known as the *esusu*, among the Yoruba of south-

[19] Polly Hill, *The Migrant Cocoa-Farmers of Southern Ghana* (Cambridge: At the University Press, 1963), pp. 179-80 and 218.

western Nigeria. According to him, the *esusu* is "one of the economic institutions of the Yoruba of Nigeria, [having] elements which resemble a credit union, an insurance scheme and a savings club, but it is distinct from all of these. The *esusu* is a fund to which a group of individuals make fixed contributions of money at fixed intervals; the total amount contributed by the entire group is assigned to each of the members in rotation."[20]

The *esusu* per se is not a product of regional mobility, but there is evidence that it has been transmitted through this medium and adopted by other communities. In his study of Onitsha market, for instance, J. O. C. Onyeme-lukwe found that although the *esusu* was organized by Yoruba immigants, most of the members of the *esusu* group were Ibo traders.[21] He pointed out that one reason given by these traders for joining is that experience has taught them that such organizations were more likely to be conducted honestly when undertaken by migrants. Apart from this evidence from Iboland, there are clear suggestions of diffusion of this method of capital formation through the name given it in different parts of West Africa. In Freetown, Sierra Leone, for instance, it is known as *asusu*; in Kumasi, Ghana, as *susu*; and among the Ibibio of south-eastern Nigeria as *osusu*. These names are very close to the Yoruba *esusu* and are probably suggestive of diffusion from that source or from the same source. One should not, however, stress this point too much, since the institution is known by other names elsewhere in West Africa. Among the Hausa of Northern

---

20 William R. Bascom, "The *Esusu*: A Credit Institution of the Yoruba," *Journal of the Royal Anthropological Institute*, 82, pt. 1 (1952): 63.

21 J. O. C. Onyemelukwe, "Staple Food Trade in Onitsha Market: An Example of Urban Market Distribution Function" (Seminar Paper, Department of Geography, University of Ibadan, 1967).

Nigeria, for instance, it is known as *adaski*; among the Fang of southern Cameroons as *djana*; in Dahomey as *ndjonu*; and in Porto Novo as *tontines*.[22] Moreover, as Clifford Geertz has pointed out, similar organizations are to be found in many other parts of the underdeveloped world outside of West Africa.[23] It would appear that their development in the West Indies, for example, came with the arrival of slaves from West Africa.

Nonetheless, it is possible to appreciate the significance of introducing this method of small-scale capital formation into a new area. When the monthly contribution collected by members in rotation is not immediately disbursed in the conspicuous consumption often demanded for funerals, weddings, or similar social occasions, there are indications it is invested in some economic venture which may stimulate resource development in the area. There have been very few quantitative studies of the uses to which proceeds, accruing from membership with such credit associations, have been put. For those interested in economic development, this is a research area that could yield tremendous insight into development processes in the underdeveloped countries.

DIFFUSION OF MATERIAL OBJECTS

Specific objects and traits have also been transferred through regional mobility. Perhaps in no area of resource development is this type of impact from regional mobility felt more strongly than in agriculture. Contrary to popular opinion, farmers in West Africa are particularly keen on experimenting with new crops or new varieties of crops. As such, returning migrants have tremendous

22 Little, *West African Urbanization*, pp. 51-52.
23 Clifford Geertz, "The Rotating Credit Association: A 'Middle Rung' in Development," *Economic Development and Cultural Change*, 10, no. 3 (April 1962): 241-63.

importance in that they have brought back new seeds to their home areas. No crops show this fact better than cassava and cocoa, both of which have been introduced into West Africa from South America and today virtually dominate large areas of the agricultural landscape.

Cassava

The story of the spread of cassava (or manioc) from its original source region in Brazil to large parts of West Africa has been impressively documented by William O. Jones.[24] He saw this dispersion in particular as one of the effects of cultural contacts between Europe and Africa which, although relatively undramatic, has resulted in fundamental changes in the economic landscape of the continent. Cassava was originally domesticated by the South American Indians and was introduced to Africa by the Portuguese soon after the discovery of America in the fifteenth century. The Portuguese extended its distribution in South America because of its value in provisioning their stations along the Brazilian coast. They also introduced it to their stations along the west coast of Africa, notably on Sao Tome and in the Kingdom of the Congo. By 1700, cassava was already an important food crop in Sao Tome and Principe. Although it was already known to the Africans living in the Niger Delta, it seems not to have been important on the mainland at that time. Indeed, it would appear that there was then some resistance to its adoption over most of West Africa.

Jones suggests that one reason for the initial resistance to the adoption of cassava is its poisonous character if it is not properly prepared. If cassava is handled in the

24 See William O. Jones, "Manioc: An Example of Innovation in African Economics," *Economic Development and Cultural Change*, 5, no. 2 (January 1957): 97-117, and Jones, *Manioc in Africa* (Stanford, Calif.: Stanford University Press, Food Research Institute, 1959).

same way as the more traditional yam crop, it contains dangerous amounts of prussic acid. A few unfortunate incidents with this new food plant were thus sufficient to discourage its use for many years. In fact, it appears that the subsequent adoption of the crop was due to a re-introduction of both the crop and the process of making a meal out of it. The agency for this re-introduction was a number of freed slaves migrating back from Brazil to West Africa from about 1780 onwards. These returning Africans formed an important trading class, and their prestige and influence in places like Lagos and Abomey were very high. Le Herissé mentioned, for instance, that an old Dahomey chief interviewed by him about 1910 asserted that his people had been taught how to prepare cassava so that they could eat it without becoming ill. Their teacher had been the first "Chancha," the name given to the famous Brazilian, Francisco Felix da Souza, when he first came to West Africa in 1788.[25]

Adanson in 1750 also reported cassava as a crop growing well in the Gambia and, in the 1790s, Mungo Park saw it growing in gardens near towns and villages along the lower Gambia River.[26] From these coastal centres, the cultivation of cassava spread over a large part of West Africa (fig. 11). According to Jones, the area planted with this crop made up, by 1950, about 40 per cent of all land in food crops in this part of the world. All indications are that the crop will continue to increase in importance and that more land will be devoted to its cultivation.

25 A. Le Herissé, *L'Ancien Royaume du Dahomey* (Paris: E. Larose, 1911), p. 324.

26 M. Adanson, "A Voyage to Senegal, the Isle of Goree, and the River Gambia," in John Pinkerton, ed., *A General Collection of the Best and Most Interesting Voyages in All Parts of the World*, vol. 16 (London: Longman, Hurst, Rees & Orme, and Cadell & Davies, 1814), pp. 598-674, and Mungo Park, *Travels in the Interior Districts of Africa*, vol. 1 (London: John Murray, 1816), pp. 13-14.

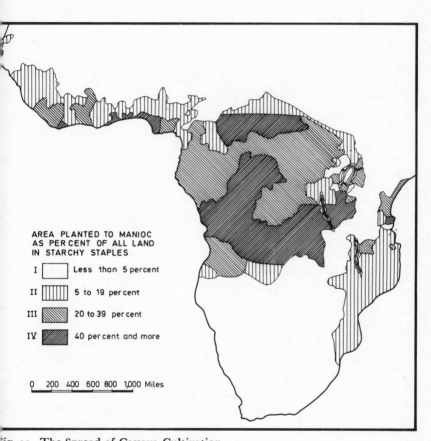

AREA PLANTED TO MANIOC
AS PER CENT OF ALL LAND
IN STARCHY STAPLES

I   Less than 5 percent

II   5 to 19 per cent

III   20 to 39 per cent

IV   40 per cent and more

0   200   400   600   800   1,000 Miles

Fig. 11. The Spread of Cassava Cultivation

SOURCE: William O. Jones, *Manioc in Africa* (Stanford, Calif.: Stanford University Press, Food Research Institute, 1959), p. 58.

The crucial question from our point of view is, of course, how the crop came to spread over such a wide area of West Africa. In this respect, Jones emphasized the role of regional mobility. He suggested that the pre-disposing condition to its spread, especially after 1900, was the rapid increase in population and the consequent shortening of the fallow period. The latter meant a de-cline in soil fertility and in the productivity of tradi-tional crops such as yams. Once this happened, it was relatively easy to introduce cassava as a crop that could grow on soils too impoverished for other staples. With the establishment of cassava cultivation on the coast, its spread inland was brought about by the large number of migratory workers moving to and fro across West Africa.

L. C. Uzozie, writing on the relative importance of yam and cassava in the staple food economies of Eastern Nigeria, provided more detailed information on the mechanism of spread within a limited area. [27] According to him, information supplied by old people suggests that the main agency of transfer of cassava from the Ijaws and Ogoni people of the Niger Delta into the Ibo hinterland were the Aro. They were reported to have brought the crop to Okigwi and to a number of other settlements. Itinerant Hausa and Awka blacksmiths were also associ-ated with the spread of the crop in the Abakaliki and Owerri provinces respectively.

An important element of the spread was, no doubt, the willingness of local farmers to try the new crops on their land. The Reverend Henry Townsend, writing about Egba farmers in 1850, remarked on this trait among African farmers. He noted that "the people are fond of obtaining new fruit trees, as well as varieties of

[27] L. C. Uzozie, "The Relative Importance of Yams and Cassava in the Staple Food Economies of Eastern Nigeria" (M.A. thesis, University of Ibadan, 1966), p. 30.

vegetables and fruits that they already have. The yam, which is a staple article of food and commerce with them, they possess in great varieties and new sorts they are ever seeking to obtain from adjacent countries."[28] Uzozie also attested to the importance of this trait among the farmers. He emphasized that once the cultivation of a new plant was adopted by a village, the mechanism of its spread among the people was simple. The market place was a forum for the transmission of new ideas. A new crop growing in a neighbour's farm would certainly constitute a curiosity. Indeed, there was a case in Iboland in which a farmer was said to have stolen a high-yielding cassava variety from a neighbour's farm and to have been fined the sum of twenty pounds for so doing. In consequence of this incident, the cassava variety is known locally as *Ohupon*, an Ibo word meaning "twenty pounds."[29]

In many parts of West Africa, the local names for cassava can often be indicative of the circumstances of its introduction, the place from which it was obtained, or the incidents in village life in which it has figured. The important thing to stress, however, is that this spectacular spread of cassava has been largely the product of the considerable mobility of people within West Africa. Only recently, a research worker in the northern part of Western Nigeria reported the enthusiastic adoption of a new variety of cassava which matures in six months instead of the usual nine months.[30] The new variety was

28 Reverend Henry Townsend, *Journals*, Church Missionary Society, Salisbury Square, London, CA2/085, June 1850.

29 See M. J. Ekandem, *Cassava in Nigeria: Eastern Nigeria*, Moor Plantation Memorandum no. 42 (Ibadan, Nigeria: Federal Department of Agricultural Research, December 1962), pp. 5-6, and Jones, *Manioc in Africa*, p. 99.

30 A. Adegbola, "The Impact of Migration on Economy: The Example of Oshun Division, Western Nigeria" (Ph.D. thesis, University of Ibadan, 1971).

brought back from the Ivory Coast by a trader who operates between the two areas.

Cocoa

The same story of the effect of regional mobility on resource development can be told with respect to the tremendous expansion of cocoa cultivation in West Africa. As with cassava, cocoa was initially introduced to West Africa from the New World by the Portuguese. The Portuguese are reputed to have planted cocoa on the island of Sao Tome as far back as 1822, although it was not until about 1870 that they concentrated seriously on its cultivation.[31] By then, cultivation was also spreading apace in the neighbouring island of Fernando Po. This island has the distinction of depending for much of its labour on people from the mainland. A few of these returning labourers have been credited with having introduced the crops into different parts of West Africa.

K. D. Dickson suggested that two unsuccessful attempts had been made in Ghana to encourage the peasant farmers to grow cocoa before the arrival back of Tetteh Quashie from Fernando Po in 1876.[32] The first of these would appear to have been by the Dutch at Elmina around 1800; the second by the Basel Mission at Akropong between 1857 and 1866. Tetteh Quashie's innovative crop, by contrast, seemed to have caught on almost immediately. He had brought back from Fernando Po a few cocoa pods with which he made a farm at Mampong in Akwapim. So successful was the farm that, by 1883, he was already selling cocoa pods at £1 each and cocoa seedlings at 2s. 6d. to neighbouring farmers eager to try out the new crop. The first export consignment

31 F. N. Howes, "The Early Introduction of Cocoa to West Africa," *African Affairs*, 45, no. 180 (July 1946): 152-53.

32 K. D. Dickson, "Cocoa in Ghana" (Ph.D. thesis, University of London, 1960), p. 87.

from his farm in 1885 weighed 121 pounds and was valued at just over £6. From this small beginning grew the cocoa industry on which the economic development of Ghana rests so heavily today.

Nonetheless, the most impressive part of the saga of the cocoa industry in Ghana was the rapidity of its spread away from Akwapim. All writers on the subject have commented on the important role played by the mobility of Akwapim and Krobo farmers. We have already discussed some of the institutional innovations resulting from the movements of these people, and it is now necessary to stress that not only were they buying up lands, but they were, at the same time, introducing a new crop into the agricultural landscape of most of the areas into which they moved. In these areas, they were known to have sold the crops to local farmers and, in some cases, to have shown the farmers how to grow these crops. Indeed, so important is the movement of these people for the development of the cocoa industry, that Polly Hill was tempted to suggest that "the rapid expansion of cocoa-growing always involves migration" and that the Akwapim, like other groups in West Africa that have taken up extensive cocoa cultivation, had what she called a "mobile agricultural outlook."[33]

This point of view seems to find some support in the development of cocoa cultivation in the Ivory Coast. Marguerite Dupire, in her very interesting study on indigenous and stranger farmers in the south-eastern Ivory Coast, calls attention to the important role of the stranger farmers in cocoa production in this country.[34] The earliest group of these migrant planters were the Diula, a subgroup of the Malinke who played important roles

[33] Hill, *Migrant Cocoa-Farmers of Southern Ghana*, p. 169.
[34] Marguerite Dupire, "Planteurs autochtones et étrangers en Basse-Côte d'Ivoire Orientale," *Etudes Eburnéennes*, 8 (1960): 7-237.

as traders all over these parts of West Africa. When, by 1916, they found that cocoa cultivation was an increasingly profitable investment, a number of them began to buy land and establish plantations in the relatively empty forest areas of the south-eastern Ivory Coast. They were followed by numerous other Malinke from the north, so that nowadays migrant planters predominate in some of the areas which they "opened up." Dupire, in fact, found that strangers outnumbered indigenous inhabitants in the Abe village of Rubino and in the Agni village of Assouba. In Rubino, moreover, the strangers' plantations were considerably more extensive than those of the local Abe. Figure 12 shows in more detail their position in the canton of Assouba. There were at least fifteen large villages of migrant farmers compared to four (Eniambo, Assouba, Ayebo, and Adaou) of the local Agni population.

Sarah Berry suggests that Western Nigeria is an exception to the rule. In this area, she suggests, cocoa has been planted almost entirely by Yorubas on Yoruba territory. The Yorubas have not migrated to lands occupied by other people, nor have strangers established cocoa plantations in Yorubaland.[35] This suggestion, however, can have only partial validity, since it does not deny the importance of regional mobility for the introduction of the crop. Berry herself recorded that some of the earliest planters remembered by farmers in the area she studied were people who, like Tetteh Quashie in Ghana, had travelled outside Yorubaland and there became acquainted with the crop. One of these, for instance, " a Mr. Ogunwole, had served with the French army in Porto

[35] Sarah Berry, "Cocoa in Western Nigeria, 1890–1940. A Study of an Innovation in a Developing Economy" (Ph.D. thesis, University of Michigan, Ann Arbor, 1967).

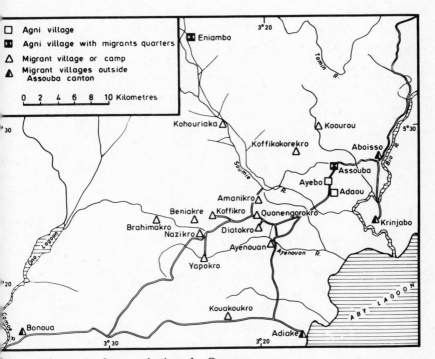

Fig. 12. Migrant Settlements in Assouba Country

SOURCE: Marguerite Dupire, "Planteurs autochtones et étrangers en Base-Côte d'Ivoie Orientale," *Etudes Eburnéennes*, 8 (1960): 179.

Novo where he first encountered cocoa. After being discharged, he returned to Ibadan bringing with him 200 cocoa pods which he had bought near Lagos and which he planted at his village just northeast of Ibadan. His example apparently encouraged other Ibadan people to try the new crop and he supplied some with seed."[36] Another early planter in the Ibadan area was said to have been a sailor who decided to retire from his sailing career and join his brother to farm at the village of Onipe. He brought cocoa seeds with him which the villagers thought he had acquired during his travels, perhaps in Sierra Leone or the Gold Coast, although he might only have seen the seeds growing in those places. Later, the spread of crops in many cases was due to the activities of Christian missionaries and itinerant traders as well as of farmers searching for new, unused lands. The important point then is not that regional mobility played no part in the growth of the cocoa industry in Western Nigeria, but that it was limited to the early phase of introducing the crop. Subsequent expansion was undertaken largely by the indigenes themselves.

It is possible to multiply examples of crops, objects, and traits whose wide use or cultivation have been due largely to the effect of regional mobility. In essence, much of the role of traders in distant markets falls into the same category. When Yoruba traders carry local craft goods from their home area to distant markets, they stimulate a demand for these goods which eventually must have an effect on production of both the raw materials and the craft goods in their home areas. When returning migrants bring back from distant places plants, tools, or goods for which they manage to generate local

[36] For this story, Berry cites J. A. Ayorinde, "Historical Notes on the Introduction and Development of the Cocoa Industry in Western Nigeria," *Nigerian Agricultural Journal*, 3, no. 1 (April 1966): 19.

demand, the consequence of their movement must result in some resource development either in their home area or in the land of their temporary sojourn.

There are two important points to stress concerning the migrant's contribution to resource development. In a situation where neither highly developed agricultural extension services nor sophisticated trade promotional activities exists, his role could be crucial. Also, because he occupies a special position within his own community, the community is inclined to accept most of his innovative activities. He is the person who has been to different places and who now knows various ways of doing things. Usually, he is attracted to trying those projects that he has seen succeed in another area. Consequently, he attempts his innovation often with a most infectious confidence that can be crucial in ensuring success and stimulating its adoption by others.

DISSEMINATION OF CULTURAL VALUES

Finally, there is an aspect of regional mobility which, though intangible, often has great significance for resource development. This is the dissemination of those cultural values which are prerequisites for the economic success of migrants. Let me stress again that I am not concerned with the seasonal or short-term labour migrants who are, par excellence, the product of the colonial era. Rather, I am concerned with the type of migrant who, in essence, represents a continuation of a pre-colonial tradition of mobility, one who moves around in search of opportunities and responds effectively to these when they beckon. Such a migrant, having left his home area, often operates with a certain singleness of purpose — the acquisition of wealth. This singleness of mind means the deprecation of any social fetters which may prevent him from doing any particular type of job which he identifies as important for the achievement of his purpose. Away from his home area, he can also ignore relatively easily any such social constraint. His single-mindedness invariably means a devotion to hard work, an acceptance of long hours of work, and working all days of the week if necessary. More than this, he is responsive to business or economic opportunities and is prepared to try his hand at a variety of enterprises in the hope of finally settling down on whichever turns out to be the most successful.

And the truth is that many migrants do succeed at least on some modest scale. What is not always clear is the effect of their success on the indigenous population. Unfortunately, favourable references by local leaders to the need for their people to absorb some of these values so successfully demonstrated by the migrant population are not always regarded as newsworthy. Nor are the many instances recorded when individuals themselves have gone or sent their children to learn from immigrants new ways of doing things. When I was a boy in Kano, Nigeria, it used to be the practice for Nigerian parents to send their children to live with migrants from Sierra Leone in the hope that they would thereby learn certain types of skills and the discipline needed for success in modern circumstances. In other places, parents sent their daughters to live with and work for migrant women traders in the hope that they would learn the intricate art of successful trading.

It is said that what often catches the attention of historians are the conflicts between the migrant and the local population, the odd instance when a member of the local population has resented the wealth or show of wealth of a migrant, or the situations created when previously cordial relations have been allowed to degenerate so much as to threaten the peace and stability of the whole community. Nonetheless, there is some evidence that regional mobility has been instrumental in spreading those values which are vital for the stimulation of development in many parts of West Africa.

Conclusion

I have indicated in this chapter that resource development has followed from regional mobility in a direct and in an indirect way. Direct resource development covers those situations where increased production of an agricultural crop or a craft good can be shown to follow from the innovative activities of migrants. Indirect resource development embraces those ideas, techniques, or institutions devised by migrants in response to needs generated by regional mobility and which can be shown to affect the rate and stability of that portion of resource development attributable to these migrants. And, although many of these ideas, techniques, and institutions have been studied in the past, especially in a sociological context, there is an increasing need for research aimed at gaining more insight into their significance for economic development.

In a community where agencies for resource development, such as agricultural extension services, sales promotional services, and widespread advertisement facilities, are non-existent or poorly developed, migrants are important because they are able to perform these functions. That regional mobility continues to be significant may be related to the general low level of developmental response that these modern agencies have been able to generate at the present time. For societies where the presence of an agricultural research institute has no meaningful significance, where illiteracy makes advertisement through the printed word non-accessible, and where confidence is not easily generated by impersonal communication, the role of migrants with their immediacy of contact can easily be seen to be crucial.

Maybe, as Elliot Berg suggests for the colonial labour migration, regional mobility of the type described here will disappear as the specific set of economic circumstances that have given rise to it gradually changes; for instance, if education were to become more universal and industrialization more pervasive in the area.[37] On the other hand, it is possible to conceive that regional mobility may also change its essential features to meet the challenges of these new situations. Whatever happens, it is necessary to be aware of the important role which the relative freedom of movement of West African people has played in the development of the area up to now.

It is true that it has not been possible to quantify the significance of regional mobility to resource development. There are no data to show what proportion of agricultural or fish output has been due to the efforts of immigrants, to show the volume of local craft goods moving into distant countries as a result of the activities of immigrant traders, or to indicate investment activities resulting from income to migrants in their land of sojourn. But it is also true that as one surveys the literature, leafs through historical documents, or listens to responses to interview questions, one is very conscious of the fact that so much in the development of West Africa is owed to people who did not hesitate to take their lives in their hands and venture to distant lands, or who, whilst there, found new and exciting ways of doing things and were not afraid to try them out locally or back in their home areas.

37 Elliot J. Berg, "The Economics of the Migrant Labour System," in Hilda Kuper, ed., *Urbanization and Migration in West Africa* (Berkeley: University of California Press, 1965), p. 175.

CHAPTER IV:
REGIONAL MOBILITY IN THE CHANGING POLITICAL SCENE

IN THIS FINAL CHAPTER, I return to the theme of the transitional character of the political and economic conditions in West Africa, and I will emphasize the aspects of the political scene. In Chapter 1, I indicated that West Africa must be seen as emerging from a pre-national, pre-industrial situation into a national, pre-industrial state, which is already striving towards a national, industrial position. This remarkably fluid situation is of crucial importance for appreciating the significance and prospects of regional mobility in the whole region.

BACKGROUND TO THE POLITICAL SCENE

To identify the background with the present situation, one must examine the prelude to the colonial period when Britain, France, Portugal, and Germany, rather than divide West Africa into four broad areas so that each could take their one-quarter share, partitioned it into fourteen uneven trading spheres of influence. This checkerboard pattern remained even when Germany was removed from the scene. France and Britain came to dominate the whole area, and Portugal was confined to the small and single territory of Portuguese Guinea. Thus, by the period of independence starting from 1957, France had nine territories in West Africa, Britain had four, and Portugal one. There was also the independent state of Liberia.

This division of West Africa into a patchwork of trading areas and later of colonial territories can thus be criticized as not being wholly rational. Indeed, it is to this aspect of the colonial period that we owe the existence of so many mini-states in West Africa today. Three of these states have populations of under one million, ten have populations of under five million, one has under ten million, and only one country has a population of over ten million. This smallness of size, it will be shown later, is not unimportant when an explanation of the attitude of many of the new states to regional mobility is considered. Nonetheless, it is important to stress that even the smallest of the colonial territories was larger than the area occupied by many ethnic groups in West Africa. In other words, this patchwork of colonial territories, in spite of its irrationality, represented a high order of unification, especially in those parts of West Africa that had never been integrated into any of the former indigenous empires and kingdoms. Thus, even in their smallness, all the West African states are multi-ethnic and multi-lingual.

Another criticism of the colonial adventure by European countries into Africa is that the boundaries which they drew to delimit the territory under their control had no regard for the convenience of the local peoples. Most of the boundaries divided ethnic groups and placed them under two or even more administrations. K. M. Barbour pointed out that political boundaries in West Africa cut through the lands of nearly one hundred ethnic groups. But he also emphasized that where the drawing of boundaries was known as being likely to create unnecessary inconvenience to the local people, the

116

colonial powers in a number of instances agreed to waive the significance of the boundary.[1] Thus, in the Anglo-French agreement of 11 May 1905, concerning the boundary between the Gold Coast and the adjoining territory, it was provided that "the villages situated in proximity to the frontier shall retain the right to use the arable and pasture lands, springs and watering places which they have heretofore used," even if these lay in the other's territory.[2] These rather extensive boundary-making activities were, almost by mutual consent, allowed to have no overriding effect with respect to people living close to the border. As a result, there was, throughout the colonial period, continuous coming and going across the frontiers, especially by farmers who did not need to carry any formal papers.

Against these two criticisms, there was a positive integrative attempt by the colonial powers to treat these various territories as if they were a single political unit. Apart from providing similar systems of administration and education, the colonial powers strove to facilitate the flow of people, goods, and money among their various colonial dependencies. In the case of the French where most of these territories were contiguous, this integrative tendency was reflected even in the master-plan for railway development. The basic idea behind this was not so much to provide a network for each of the territories but to link the interior areas with the coast through four lines planned to go from specific points on the coast to the river Niger. As was pointed out earlier, two lines did

1 K. M. Barbour, "A Geographical Analysis of Boundaries in Intertropical Africa," in K. M. Barbour and R. Mansell Prothero, eds. *Essays on African Population* (London: Routledge and Kegan Paul, 1961), pp. 312-13.

2 E. Hertslet, *The Map of Africa by Treaty*, 3rd ed., vol. 2 (1909; rpt., London: Frank Cass, 1967), p. 841.

reach the Niger. The Abidjan-Niger reached Bobo-Dioulasso in 1934 and was extended to Ouagadougou in 1945.
The Benin-Niger reached Parakou in 1936.

Although the railway was originally intended to link
the interior areas with the coast, it also became a major
channel for the movement of people and goods among
the various French West African territories. A large
proportion of immigrants coming into the Ivory Coast
during the migration survey taken in 1959 came by rail.
However, whether they came by rail or by other means,
entry conditions were very lax, and there was no question of a resident or work permit. Especially with African members of the Colonial Civil Service, France made
no distinction about their territory of origin and was
prepared to transfer them to any of the colonies. This
was particularly true of Senegalese and Dahomeans, two
coastal peoples who had benefited most from the colonial
educational system. Functionaries of Senegalese origin
were thus sent to work in centres all over French West
Africa whilst those from Dahomey were to be found
especially in Niger and Upper Volta.[3]

But perhaps more important in its integrative role was
the uniform currency system operated in all the territories. Indeed, until 1945, the French monetary system
prevailed throughout the colonial territories. Though
issued locally by the Banque de L'Afrique Occidentale
Française (BAO), the colonial franc had the same value
as the franc that circulated in France. In 1945, however,
"on the ground that the economic consequences of the
Second World War justified a sharp devaluation of the
national currency in France but not in colonial Africa,
a new CFA (Colonies Françaises d'Afrique) franc" was

3 Virginia Thompson and Richard Adloff, *French West Africa* (London: Allen & Unwin, 1958), p. 200.

established with its value fixed at roughly twice the metropolitan franc. What needs to be stressed is the fact that in all these changes, the French West African territories were treated as a single unit. Moreover, the Banque de L'Afrique Occidentale Française which, although a commercial bank, had the exclusive privilege of issuing paper money, had set up branches in all the colonies soon after 1901.[4]

These facts imply that wherever a migrant might move within the French colonial territories in West Africa, he had no problem of currency conversion, exchange control, or transfer of funds. It is perhaps a measure of the abiding French influence in these territories, or perhaps a factor of their contiguity, that even after independence these territories, except for Guinea and Mali, have chosen to retain the same monetary system, although they have changed the meaning of the letters CFA to Communauté Financière Africaine.[5] It is too early to say how long this uniformity will last in the face of divergent economic policies and social programmes. What is clear is that its existence since colonial times has been a major factor facilitating regional mobility and thereby stimulating resource development.

When we turn to the British colonial territories in West Africa, we find a position not basically different. Because of a lack of contiguity, there was little prospect of an integrated transport network. The civil service, however, was fairly open to persons from any of the colonial territories who had the necessary skills and training. In consequence, large numbers of Sierra Leoneans were to be found in administrative positions in Nigeria,

4 Ibid., pp. 277-81.
5 See "A West African Franc?" *West Africa*, no. 2308 (26 August 1961): 939.

Ghana, and Gambia. Sierra Leone had had the benefit of post-secondary education from the second half of the nineteenth century when Fourah Bay College was established, and was thus in a position to provide this level of manpower to the other British West African territories. Much later, Ghana too came to supply Nigeria with a sizeable amount of trained manpower. More than this, non-civil servants such as traders, artisans, and labourers moved from one to the other of these territories and settled down to work with the minimum of let or hindrance.

But just as in the case of French West Africa, the existence of a common currency and of an inter-territorial banking system was an important element in the movement. The background to this development was the formation in 1894 of the Bank of British West Africa as a result of the initiative of G. W. Neville and Sir Alfred Lewis Jones. Initially, "this bank, by organizing the importation and exportation of currency, and providing banking services, made no small contribution to the growth of a monetary economy" in all four British colonial territories in West Africa.[6] Eventually in 1912, its currency issuing function was taken over by the West African Currency Board which operated a common currency in the four territories until, with its independence in 1957, Ghana contracted out. Nigeria also contracted out in 1958 and so did Sierra Leone in 1963.[7] While it lasted, the West African Currency Board facilitated the transfer of funds to and from any of the territories, and the parity of money which it ensured was of great benefit

[6] W. T. Newlyn and D. C. Rowan, *Money and Banking in British Colonial Africa* (Oxford: At The Clarendon Press, 1954), p. 26.

[7] See Charles V. Brown, *The Nigerian Banking System* (Evanston, Ill.: Northwestern University Press, 1966), p. 52, and R. G. Saylor, *The Economic System of Sierra Leone* (Durham, N.C.: Duke University Press, 1967), p. 177.

to all those involved in regional mobility between the areas.

NATIONHOOD AND THE CITIZENSHIP CRISIS

The end of World War II marked the beginning of a process which was to lead to the decolonization of West Africa and to the rise of new, independent nation-states. The first of these new states, apart from Liberia, was Ghana which became independent in 1957. Within the next four years, all the British and French colonies except Gambia had become independent.

Almost as soon as they became independent, these states, in asserting their new identity, began to break up the integrated colonial system. This was particularly so in the case of the British West African territories. The independent state of Ghana contracted out of not only the West African Currency Board but also the West African Airways and the West African Research Organisation. In each case, it proceeded to set up its own institutions. The other countries, as they too became independent, followed the Ghanaian example, almost by necessity. In the French West African territories, the process did not go as far. Guinea broke completely from the French orbit, and the Mali Federation of Senegal and Soudan (Français) did not last very long. Nor did other attempts at integration have any more success. The Ghana-Guinea Union, formed in 1958, proved to be short-lived. The Conseil de l'Entente formed in 1959 and comprising Ivory Coast, Upper Volta, Dahomey, and Niger (Togo was induced to join in 1965) provided in its agreement for a customs union, but to date its achievements in economic matters have been negligible.[8]

8 Peter Robson, *Economic Integration in Africa* (London: Allen & Unwin, 1968), p. 17.

The only exception to the rule is the Cameroons where the political union of former British and French territories is showing evidence of being stable and workable.[9]

From the point of view of the migrants, however, the real significance of national independence was the fact that for the first time the various countries had to define who were its citizens and who were not. This issue is one which, in many West African countries, quickly becomes shrouded in controversy and contradictions. Ghana provides the best example of the type of problems involved. What follows here has been taken direct from the issues of the weekly newspaper *West Africa* (now published in Lagos) which covered the events at the time.[10] In the colonial period, a distinction was sometimes made between "natives" and "non-natives." The latter supposedly comprised members of groups which territorially lie outside the boundaries of the then Gold Coast. However, the term "natives" was legally defined as "British subjects or protected persons." According to British law (British Nationality and Status of Aliens Act, 1914), a British subject was anyone born "within His Majesty's dominions and allegiance." This law prevailed until the time of Ghanaian independence when the British Nationality Act of 1948 declared that British citizenship could be lost by the acquisition of Ghanaian citizenship.

At this point, the politics of Ghana in the pre-independence period intervened and influenced the terms of the Ghanaian Nationality Act. In the preliminaries to independence, many migrants became involved in poli-

9 For information on the success so far achieved, see Edwin Ardener, "The Nature of the Reunification of Cameroon," in Arthur Hazlewood, ed., *African Integration and Disintegration* (London: Oxford University Press, 1967), pp. 285-337.

10 "Muslims and Citizens," *West Africa*, no. 2684 (9 November 1968): 1311-12.

tical activity. Their support was sought by all parties, and they were encouraged to vote and participate in politics. As the Convention People's Party (CPP) of Dr. Kwame Nkrumah gained power and the opposition to the CPP in some areas, notably Kumasi, was actively supported by the heads of various "stranger communities" such as the Hausa, Yoruba, Mossi, and Gao, attempts were made to prevent immigrants from voting. These occurred as early as 1954, but until independence such attempts remained unofficial. In 1957, two prominent strangers, the late Alhaji Amadu Baba, the Serikin Zongo of Kumasi, and Alhaji Othman Lalemie, also of Kumasi, were deported. Although of Hausa origin, both men had been born in Ghana and had tried to argue in court that they were Ghanaian citizens. "We do not say that we are natives of Ghana as such; in this struggle we are not fighting for ourselves alone, but we are fighting for many thousands of Nigerians who were born in Ghana and whose parents were born there. Our contention is that we and they are citizens of Ghana by birth. If we fail in this struggle they will fail and that is why we are determined to establish our right of citizenship."[11] In order to "legalize" their deportations, a special act, the Deportation Act of 1957, was passed while their case was being heard in Kumasi. Before the termination of the court proceedings, the men were removed to Nigeria.

At this time, the Ghana Nationality and Citizenship Act of 1957 (Act 1 of May 1957) was passed. According to this act, birth in Ghana did not confer citizenship. A person's parents or grandparents had to be born in Ghana for birth to confer citizenship. This act was repealed by Act 62 of 1961, but the law remained basically the same. Consequently from 1957 to 1967, many second

11 "Two Alhajis Deported from Ghana Are Flown to Kano," *West Africa*, no. 2107 (31 August 1957): 831.

generation immigrants in Ghana were without any African nationality, although legally those born in Ghana before independence remained British.

During the past ten years, the embassies of the surrounding countries, as they too achieved independence, began issuing identity cards to the Ghanaian-born children of immigrants from their countries. Organizations such as the Upper Volta Union and the Nigerian Community were formed in association with embassies and high commissions, and the nationalist sympathies of immigrants in Ghana were increasingly focused on the countries of their forefathers.

Since the coup in February 1966, the Ghana Nationality Act has been amended by the Ghana Nationality Decree 1967 (NLCD 191). According to this new decree, virtually everyone born in Ghana is a citizen by birth. Consequently, as long as embassies continue issuing identity cards to second generation immigrants, these people could have dual, or alternative, allegiances. In Ghana, the commissioner responsible for citizenship may lawfully deprive a Ghanaian of citizenship when that person has obtained citizenship in another country. The situation is thus potentially difficult for immigrants, since they are liable to lose citizenship rights entirely or they may be accused of "playing it both ways."

The position in Ghana thus shows clearly the current constitutional vicissitudes of the migrant. What it does not show are the economic and social hazards that are now increasingly part of the lot of sojourners abroad, whether or not they live in countries where rights of citizenship are accorded to them. A review of the growing list of some of the specific anti-stranger events in the last ten years in different parts of West Africa would unmistakably demonstrate this point.

DISCRIMINATORY ACTS AGAINST MIGRANTS

Dahomey is one country that has felt most the impact of what Ali A. Mazrui referred to as "a retreat from Pan-Africanism."[12] This country was the most educationally advanced of French colonial territories in West Africa; as such, it had supplied most of these territories as well as French Equatorial Africa and even Belgian Congo with skilled manpower such as doctors, teachers, clerks, and traders. As the movement towards independence gathered momentum, the presence of Dahomeans in all these positions began to attract unfavourable attention. In October 1958, on the alleged suspicion of a new influx of Dahomean and Togolese immigrants, there was a violent outbreak in Abidjan, capital of the Ivory Coast, in which one man was killed, fifty others injured, and several houses were damaged. In consequence, more than one thousand Togolese and Dahomean men and women left the Ivory Coast to return to their homes.[13]

Again in 1963, over a dispute with Dahomey, Niger suddenly ordered all Dahomeans living in its territory, estimated at about sixteen thousand, to leave the country before the end of the year. Later, in 1964, it agreed to expel only Dahomean civil servants and not all Dahomeans, as had been threatened. It also agreed to space the expulsion in order to avoid disruption in the economy of the two countries.[14]

Nigerians in Ghana have faced similar harassments, apart from the deportation of the two Alhajis discussed

12 Ali A. Mazrui, "African Nationalism: A Re-assessment" (Paper delivered at the Twentieth Anniversary of the Program of African Studies, Northwestern University, Evanston, Illinois, September 1968).

13 "The New French Constitution," *West Africa*, no. 2168 (1 November 1958): 1041, and no. 2169 (8 November 1958): 1064.

14 "Crisis on the Niger," *West Africa*, no. 2431 (4 January 1964): 11, and no. 2443 (28 March 1964): 347.

previously. Before independence, nearly half the Africans involved in the prospecting of diamonds in Ghana were Nigerians. Many of them were legally licensed to prospect. In 1963, however, the Ghana government passed the Aliens Act which, among other things, dispossessed most Nigerians of their licences. Although many of them continued to dig diamonds, they had to do so under the aegis of Ghanaian nominal landlords![15] In most cases, it is the Nigerian who still finances the business, who pays for the licence of his new landlord as well as for the ground rent. But, because he no longer has an official existence, he cannot sell directly to the Ghana Diamond Marketing Corporation. He must sell first to his landlord who then sells to the corporation. As can be well imagined, the system has led to considerable abuse and, in particular, has facilitated tremendous opportunities for diamond smuggling out of Ghana, especially as the foreign exchange position of that country deteriorated.

More recently, in July 1968, the National Liberation Council in Ghana passed a decree which reserved five fields of economic activity to Ghanaians: taxi service operations; small-scale businesses with under thirty employees and/or investments of under 1,000 cedis; retail trade businesses with annual sales volume of less than 500,000 cedis; wholesale trade businesses with an annual sales volume of less than 1 million cedis; and representation of overseas manufacturers. According to the Economic Affairs Commissioner, foreigners in these businesses would be allowed reasonable time to wind up and make way for Ghanaians. They would no longer be issued licences to operate in any of the five protected fields; nor would they even be encouraged to participate in trading

[15] "Behind Ghana's Diamond Smuggling," *West Africa*, no. 2646 (7 February 1968): 181.

activities outside these. "The new policy, according to the Commissioner, was not aimed at general elimination of foreign entrepreneurs; but any foreigner seeking residence and employment in Ghana would have to show that he has special skills in short supply there."[16] Ten days after this decree, another decree was passed, stipulating that foreigners wishing to enter or live in certain areas of Ghana, including the diamond mining areas, must now obtain a licence. The new decree was an amendment on the 1963 Aliens Act and prescribes penalties of up to two years' imprisonment or a 500 cedi fine for infringement.

These last two decrees have affected mostly the Nigerians in Ghana. A good number of them were leaving Ghana by the end of 1968, although it is conceivable that, like migrants everywhere, a sizeable proportion would find a way around these decrees.

Ghanaians too have received similar treatment elsewhere in West Africa, notably in Sierra Leone. Ghana is known to have well over 10,000 fishing canoes and 250 inshore vessels, and her fishermen are to be found settled in large numbers in different countries on the West African coast, including Sierra Leone.[17] In December 1968, the Sierra Leone government ordered over a hundred Ghanaian fishermen to leave the country. A government statement pointed out that "there were many thousands of Ghanaian fishermen in Sierra Leone and the problem had exercised the attention of previous governments."[18] It argued that these Ghanaians excluded Sierra Leoneans from fishing and did not pay taxes; that they made beaches unsightly and unhygienic with their

16 "Ghana: Restriction on Foreign Traders," *West Africa*, no. 2667 (13 July 1968): 819, and no. 2669 (27 July 1968): 879.
17 "Fish for Ghana," *West Africa*, no. 2668 (20 July 1968): 842.
18 "Sierra Leone: Siaka and His Neighbours," *West Africa*, no. 2689 (14 December 1968): 1490.

settlements and that in so doing they damaged tourist prospects. And *West Africa* stated that, "At present, they were also a security problem in the event of attempts to infiltrate Sierra Leone from the sea. The intention of the Government was therefore to repatriate all Ghanaian fishermen, although it recognised that many were now in other occupations."[19] In response to this development, the Ghana government appointed an ad hoc committee to tackle the problem of resettling more than two thousand Ghanaian fishermen who faced expulsion from Sierra Leone.

In terms of regional mobility as defined in this study, it is also tempting to interpret the events of 1966 in Nigeria as part of the same story. After years of living and working in Northern Nigeria and of achieving a commendable measure of economic success, Ibo members of the immigrant population in the region were set upon in May and September 1966; many were killed and a large number forced to flee back to their home region. Various foreign writers have tried to explain these events as a reaction against the economic aggressiveness of the Ibos, as the product of intense ethnic antagonism against people who have been relatively more successful in their attempts at modernization. Whilst this possibility cannot be entirely ruled out as a contributory factor, it is certainly naive to ignore the very special political situations that gave rise to these events and without which the reactions to the Ibos could not have taken this particularly horrendous form.

At any rate, this short catalogue of events reflecting the changing political scene within which regional mobility takes place today must drive home the almost nostalgic strain in the remark of a Sierra Leone correspondent

19 "Sierra Leone: The Ghanaian Fishermen Affair," *West Africa*, no. 2690 (21 December 1968): 1522.

who wrote: "The benefits of colonialism were few but one advantage it did provide was freedom for all West Africans who lived under the British or French umbrellas, to live in any nearby territory which shared the same Sovereign. No people benefitted more from this freedom of movement than Sierra Leoneans and it is to our lasting pride that our forebears left Freetown to work, settle and marry in Ghana and Nigeria."[20] These are certainly sentiments which could have been voiced by many a West African migrant.

CHANGING RELATIONSHIPS

What, then, we may ask, has happened or is happening in the relationship between the migrants and the local population? Have the different ethnic groups in West Africa, accustomed to having strangers in their midst, suddenly become extremely xenophobic? Why is it becoming increasingly difficult for these new national communities to be accommodative of the stranger? Or is this a case of failure to be assimilated on the part of the migrants?

In chapter 1, I called attention to the need to take a contextual view of the processes of assimilation and accommodation. In West Africa, as in many other parts of the underdeveloped world, we have to see these processes operating within societies in a state of transition from a pre-national, pre-industrial condition to a national, industrial condition. This transitional phase of their development is important in evaluating the prospects of regional mobility. In what follows, therefore, I intend to indicate how this situation affects stranger communities all over West Africa.

David Apter and James Coleman have remarked that

20 "Director in Exile," *West Africa*, no. 2362 (8 September 1962): 992.

one of the primary challenges to the leader of a new nation is the welding of the heterogenous ethnic groups that inhabit his territory into a stable, national entity.[21] His task is to wean the populace from their primary loyalty to their ethnic group to loyalty to the new nation. To achieve this, he is prepared to bargain with local leaders over a number of public positions as well as local development of the social and economic infrastructure. The strangers collectively have no such bargaining significance. Courting their support contributes little to the goal of a stable, national entity. Moreover, there is little evidence that their loyalty to the new nation can always be relied upon, especially during a clash with the government of their home country. Furthermore, the only elements in the new nation that could have been expected to speak up for the strangers are the local communities among whom they had lived for so many years.

Yet, as Elliott P. Skinner rightly pointed out, one of the effects of the colonial period was to alter and undermine the relation between the strangers and their host communities.[22] Strangers in the pre-colonial days entered into direct relations with their hosts who sought ways and means of accommodating them within their body-politic. In the colonial period, the strangers entered these foreign areas under

> the aegis of the Europeans even when they were not directly brought by them. The result was that, unlike earlier strangers, they had only secondary relationships with the local political authorities (who were then also controlled by the Europeans) and were relatively free to deal with them as they saw

21 David E. Apter and James S. Coleman, "Pan-Africanism or Nationalism in Africa," in *Pan-Africanism Reconsidered*, ed. American Society of African Culture (Berkeley: University of California Press, 1962), p. 96.
22 Elliott P. Skinner, "Strangers in West African Societies," *Africa*, 33, no. 4 (October 1963): 307-20.

fit. Busia reports that even when the British [in Ghana] placed the strangers in Sekondi-Takoradi under the jurisdiction of the Native Authority, the strangers ignored the local authorities. He declares: "Many of the 'strangers' in the town usually have their disputes settled in arbitration by people of their own tribe, or some association or other which they have joined. But when this machinery breaks down, they resort to the District Commissioner rather than the Native Courts which many of them consider to be extortionate and not impartial."

However, it is also true to say that "some traditional authorities preferred to have the strangers deal with the Europeans. Others resented this attitude among the strangers but were powerless to do anything about it."[23]

One important point which Skinner made is that the "sheer number of strangers in foreign areas during the European colonial period was in itself also responsible for many changes in the relationship between them and the local African populations."[24] In the pre-colonial era, the stranger in West Africa depended for his livelihood on the goodwill and patronage of the host community. As such, it was vital that he understood the social system and achieved some *modus vivendi* with it. In the colonial period, he was under no such obligation. The number of strangers has itself increased considerably so that the strangers could operate as viable, self-sufficient communities on their own. A degree of parochialism vis-à-vis the local population soon developed and was easy to sustain because of the greater frequency of contacts with their home areas occasioned by the greatly improved

23 Ibid., pp. 309-10. See also K. A. Busia, *Report on a Social Survey of Sekondi-Takoradi* (London: Crown Agents for the Colonies on Behalf of the Government of the Gold Coast, 1950), pp. 67-68.
24 Skinner, p. 311.

communication and transportation network. This situation, besides, facilitated greater concern and involvement with events in their home areas and a corresponding indifference to those in the host country. Brian Stapleton, for instance, suggests that one reason why the Nigerian stranger in Ghana takes little interest in the affairs of that country is that "he does not think of himself as a permanent migrant; ties from home remain strong and some even pay taxes in their home towns in Nigeria and have voting rights there."[25] Even when strangers did take part in local activities, their participation was minimal since they continued "to regard themselves as 'strangers' having no civic responsibilities, rather than as citizens having rights and duties in the town."[26]

For ethnic strangers within the same colonial territory, the position was slightly different with respect to participation in national affairs. Often because of ease of communication, stranger communities reflected the political views of the leaders of their ethnic group back home. Where such views were very different from those of their host communities, they could and did give rise to considerable bitterness and conflict. H. L. Bretton noted that in Northern Nigeria "the *sabon garis* [strangers' quarters] of cities like Kano, for instance, are distasteful from the Hausa-Fulani point of view. Since they have many Ibo and Yoruba concentrations, they are citadels of the Ibo National Union, the NCNC, and the AG, all of which are revolutionary in terms of the prevailing Islamic order."[27]

The colonial period created a situation in which it did not matter one way or the other whether migrants to an

25 G. Brian Stapleton, "Nigerians in Ghana," *West Africa*, no. 2184 (21 February 1959): 175.

26 Busia, pp. 82-83.

27 H. L. Bretton, *Power and Stability in Nigeria* (New York: Frederick A. Praeger, 1962), p. 135.

area were socially accommodated by the host community. The position of the strangers was quite marginal to both the African and the European communities. Assimilation in terms of cultural solidarity with the host community was seen as an unwarranted exercise since, in essence, both host and stranger communities were engaged in a more vigorous process of acculturation with the European overlord. On the other hand, the instantaneous nature of transformation from a colonial territory to a nation-state meant that migrants had no time or opportunity of finding out how best to reconcile with the new political leadership. The problem was also relatively complicated by the diffused nature of this leadership, the instability of the migrants' tenure, and the lack of clarity of the social and economic goals of the new nation-states.

MIGRANTS AS ECONOMIC SCAPEGOATS

As a contrast to these disadvantages, strangers provided easy targets or whipping-boys for some of the problems of structural economic transformations that almost inevitably followed in the wake of independence. The independence movement in all these territories had been predicated on the promises by the political leaders to create better social and economic opportunities for the people. While it was easy to identify what needed to be done in the social field, at least in terms of expansion of educational and health facilities, it was more difficult to come to grips with the problems of economic development. The result was the well-known phenomenon of rising and unfulfilled expectations. Industrial development, although accepted as a basic factor in the economic transformation was, for various reasons, not growing fast enough to provide the necessary employment opportunities.

On the economic front, therefore, one major factor making continued accommodation of the immigrants increasingly difficult is the transitional, but still basically pre-industrial, nature of the economy. A pre-industrial economy, as I pointed out before, is one where only a narrow range of opportunities or resources has been developed. However, given the entrepreneurial and innovative attributes of the immigrants, it is not difficult to appreciate that they are more likely to quickly identify and come to dominate significant areas of this rather restricted resource base. On the repatriation of the Ghanaian fishermen from Sierra Leone, for instance, the *Daily Graphic* of Ghana commented: "Quite obviously the fishing industry in Sierra Leone seems to be controlled by immigrant Ghanaians. On the west coast of Africa, Ghana has the most efficient group of 'traditional' fishermen. . . . That Sierra Leonean fisherman should object to the dominance of these 'foreigners' in this particular industry is quite understandable. However, such treatment of other nationals is bound to have repercussions (however unreasonable) in the homeland of the ejected."[28]

In Ghana itself, Nigerians were being accused of dominating the diamond mining industry, taxi driving, and the retail trade. With respect to diamond mining, Stapleton remarked in 1959: "The Nigerian domination of the diamond digging industry is of especial interest. During the early forties Yorubas who were head labourers or clerks in the employ of European diggers, having saved enough money, began to obtain digging licences and concessions from Chiefs. It has been stated that 70 per cent of current licences are held by Nigerians. These

[28] Quoted in "Sierra Leone: The Ghanaian Fishermen Affair," p. 1522.

are mainly Yoruba from the Ibolo area to the south of Offa and in particular from two small towns, Inisha and Oyan in that area. The Oloyan of Oyan tells me that there are probably more of his citizens in Ghana than in Oyan itself."[29]

However, Stapleton raised what is the really crucial question about this phenomenon. "Would the diamond industry be as well developed, would its contribution to the economy be as great as it is but for the initiative of these people? Is the amount of money which, as a result, flows out of Ghana to support families in Nigeria, to build the houses, the several fine churches and the growing Grammar School in Oyan, a reasonable price to pay for Oyan business initiative?"

These are questions that need to be examined closely by most West African governments. But it is also fair to say that given the situation in most of these countries, they are questions that none of these governments can be expected to consider wholly in favour of the immigrants.

Furthermore, on the issue of transfer of funds abroad, most of the governments have been forced to take increasing cognizance of the migrants as their economies head for the hard rock of adverse balance of payments and inadequate foreign exchange. It is difficult to obtain any measure of the amount of money involved during either the colonial regime or the post-independence era. Some indication of what may be involved can be realized from the example of migrants from a single town, Shaki, in Western Nigeria. A recent study of migration from this town (table 1) showed that apart from its population of about forty thousand persons, there were to be found

29 Stapleton, p. 175.

in 1967 over ten thousand others in different countries of West Africa.[30]

TABLE 1

DISTRIBUTION OF SHAKI MIGRANTS

Country of Immigration	Males	Females	Servants and Apprentices	TOTAL
Ghana	950	1,050	500	2,500
Dahomey	700	900	200	1,800
Togo	600	700	200	1,500
Upper Volta	680	990	230	1,900
Niger	580	700	140	1,420
Ivory Coast	180	220	100	500
Mali	650	950	270	1,870
Sierra Leone	200	180	20	400
Guinea	289	401	100	790
Senegal	90	100	10	200
TOTAL	4,919	6,191	1,770	12,880

SOURCE: Financial Report of the Shaki Parapo Association Abroad, 1967.

Each of these migrants, aside from any local contribution he might make in his land of sojourn, is expected to contribute at the annual general meeting to a fund that is sent to help the development of his home town. The rate of contribution was one pound per adult employed male, ten shillings per adult employed female, and five shillings per apprentice or servant male or female (table 2).

In 1967, these contributions amounted to over eight thousand pounds. This is aside from other special levies for specific projects. The migrants were said to have contributed a large part of the cost of fifty thousand pounds

30 V. A. Adegunwa, "Shaki Migrants: Their Activities and Distribution in West Africa" (Essay, Department of Geography, University of Ibadan, June 1969).

136

TABLE 2

PUBLIC CONTRIBUTIONS OF SHAKI MIGRANTS, 1967

(in Pounds)

Country of Immigration	Males	Females	Servants and Apprentices	TOTAL
Ghana	950	525	125	1,600
Dahomey	700	450	50	1,200
Togo	600	350	50	1,000
Upper Volta	680	495	58	1,233
Niger	580	350	35	965
Ivory Coast	180	110	25	315
Mali	650	475	67	1,192
Sierra Leone	200	90	5	295
Guinea	289	201	25	515
Senegal	90	50	2	142
TOTAL	4,919	3,096	442	8,457

SOURCE: Financial Report of the Shaki Parapo Association Abroad, 1967.

for the Central Mosque and the Muslim Grammar School. They were also expected to contribute substantially to the building of the town hall, the post office, and the main roads of the town. Such transfer of funds for public purposes takes no account of remittances to meet personal obligations back home, such as children's schooling, the maintenance of aged relations, and perhaps the building of a house. All in all, one can easily see that substantial amounts of money are involved in such transfers of funds. Nonetheless, it is necessary to keep a perspective on this matter, since to be able to make such transfers at all, a migrant needs to have invested some considerable sums in his country of sojourn. For example, the two Nigerians deported from Ghana in 1957 claimed to have in that country businesses and property worth seventy thousand pounds and fifty thousand pounds respectively.

One aspect of this problem also worth stressing is that to the constraint imposed on economic development by the narrow range of resources, we must add the factor of the small size of many of the countries. This factor, whilst serving to aggravate the problem of economic competition between migrants and indigenes, also makes the only realistic solution difficult to attain. This solution is, of course, industrialization. Industrialization would not only increase employment opportunities but, by serving as an engine of growth, it would also expand the range of resources to be developed. Modern industries, however, depend to a great extent for their economic viability on the size of their markets. But because of the small size of their population and therefore their limited market potential, many West African countries have not been very successful in generating vigorous industrial development. The integration of the markets of these various small states in West Africa, which is currently being canvassed, could thus have considerable implication for mobility in the region.

The Articles of Association for such a West African Economic Community were signed by fourteen countries in Accra on 4 May 1967. These articles, however, said nothing about freedom of mobility for the people of these countries. Rather, they declare that part of the aim of the association is "to promote through the economic co-operation of member states a co-ordinated and equitable development of their economies, especially in industry, agriculture, transport and communications, trade and payments, manpower and natural resources; to further the maximum possible interchange of goods and services; to eliminate progressively customs and other barriers to the expansion of trade as well as restrictions on current payment transactions and on capital movements."[31] Nothing is said about freedom of human movement. Yet it is pertinent to examine what the prospects of regional mobility would be, whether or not a West African Economic Community is established.

PROSPECTS FOR REGIONAL MOBILITY

One can infer from the Articles of Association for a West African Economic Community, in spite of its not being mentioned specifically, that the elimination of restrictions on current payment transactions and capital movements would inevitably lead to increased mobility of people among the countries. It is difficult to see that people would be willing to transfer capital from one country to another without ensuring by their presence that this capital is judiciously utilized. What one might expect, however, is that in the future mobility will take place among people of somewhat different skills and characteristics than those involved in the present movements. However, as Nicolas Plessz pointed out, there are serious problems militating against the possible realization of an economic community in West Africa in the very near future.[32] This being so, I will turn to a consideration of the prospects for regional mobility across both ethnic and national boundaries, if the present situation continues.

With regard to mobility across ethnic lines but within any one of the new nation-states, we must accept that the imposition of new nation-states on the complex ethnic

31 United Nations, Economic and Social Council, Economic Commission for Africa, "Report of the Sub-Regional Meeting on Economic Co-operation in West Africa," Document no. E/CN. 14/366; E/CN. 14/INR/144, Annex 7 (Washington, D.C.: November 1966). Mimeographed.
32 Nicolas G. Plessz, *Problems and Prospects of Economic Integration in West Africa* (Montreal: McGill University Press, 1968), p. 79.

maps of West Africa has been and will continue to be a positive factor for regional mobility. Its effect within the national area should be the gradual reduction of the necessity for purely accommodative relations between host communities and migrants. Especially when uniform educational and legal systems, based on the use of a generally accepted official language, come to operate over the whole national area, it should be possible for a new national culture to emerge that will assimilate both the host communities and the migrants. Increasing industrialization should also facilitate this movement towards national assimilation. However, it would be naive to expect that new problems will not be created in the long and difficult process of national assimilation. But given the leadership and the will to maintain national cohesiveness, such problems within a nation-state are generally more readily resolved or kept within non-explosive dimensions.

With regard to mobility across national boundaries, one must start by recognizing that this problem has two aspects — that of the migrants and that of the country of their sojourn. From the point of view of the migrants, it is necessary to distinguish between old migrants, that is, those who are already established in foreign territories, and new migrants, those who are still to move out to these territories.

With the old migrants, I think we can expect them to endeavour by various subterfuges to continue their activities in their country of sojourn. Given their heavy social and economic investments in these countries, it is difficult to see them simply folding up and quitting. The only exception would be if they were physically removed or forced to flee as a result of violent outbreaks directed against them. Even here, their resilience and ability to stage a comeback have been most remarkable. Some indication of the more likely reaction of the old immigrants is provided by events in Ghana. Here, the immigrants were denied the right to hold diamond-digging licences in their own legal right. Rather than leave, many have simply turned round and set up Ghanaians as "fronts" for their operations. In the same way, it is difficult to see any alternatives open to them for dealing with the recent Ghanaian legislations barring them from taxi-ownership and trading. For, if they were to sell their businesses, it is not clear that they would be able to repatriate their capital, given the stringent regulations about exchange control. Similar developments have been reported from Sierra Leone where, during Sir Albert Margai's regime, restrictions were imposed on the participation of foreigners in retail trade and in certain types of business, as well as on the activities of Ghanaian fishermen. In all these instances, it is now widely alleged that many of the foreigners have evaded the restrictions by improper means.[33] These improper means include, apart from naturalizing in the country of sojourn, marrying a local girl in whose name the business continued to run, or forming a sleeping partnership with a national. With time, however, some of the more successful immigrants have reorganized their business to conform to the new national laws.

The position of new migrants would tend to be more precarious, since they can easily be kept out through refusal to issue them entry or work permits. However, since the laws tend to be rather selective (for instance, the Ghana law does not restrain the continued migration of farm labourers), it is conceivable that some migrants may come in at the agricultural level and, through frugal and austere living habits, manage to accumulate enough capital to move into other areas of the economy.

33 "Sierra Leone: End for Sir Albert?" *West Africa*, no. 2678 (28 September 1968): 1150-51.

What is certain in the case of both old and new migrants is that, until the economic conditions in most West African countries improve significantly, the difficulties of repatriating funds may lead to a gradual but significant transformation of the pattern of their investments in their country of sojourn. These changes will also lead to a slowing-down of the number of enterprising individuals and to a reduction of capital funds moving among West African countries.

From the point of view of the various governments, the prospects for regional mobility are perhaps best reflected in the words of Siaka Stevens, the prime minister of Sierra Leone. He states that, "No country can develop without its quota of foreigners, but if there is an influx of foreigners the indigenous people are deprived of their rights and privileges."[34] The three questions raised by this statement are clear: what constitutes an influx of foreigners; what are the rights and privileges of the indigenous people; and how does the presence of foreigners deprive them of these rights and privileges?

On purely quantitative grounds, it may be argued that in the case of Ghana where annual in-migration accounts for nearly 7 per cent of the total population, there is a yearly influx of foreigners into the country. But most of these are of the agricultural labour type about whom there has been very little resentment. The type of migrant who brings, apart from his labour, his capital and enterprise, would hardly form more than 1 per cent of the total population.

However, it is this small segment of the migrant population whose presence is regarded as constituting a deprivation of rights and privileges of the indigenous population. What these rights and privileges are, of course, is not clear. The rights to work hard, to trade

34 Ibid., p. 1151.

where they like, and to accumulate wealth are not for the migrants to give. Nor can the migrants take away privileges of the indigenous people to participate in the economic activities of their country or area at a level of efficiency which they choose. One is forced to conclude that behind this statement is the mercantilist assumption that the gains of the migrants are the losses of the indigenous population.

Given the oft-repeated objectives of West African governments as being the economic and resource development of their countries, two questions are therefore pertinent. Could these objectives be met by reducing the stock of enterprising individuals within their territories? Could a positive policy of stimulating and developing the competitive abilities of the indigenous people vis-à-vis the foreigners not achieve much better results than one which sees the gains of the foreigners as the loss of the indigenous people?

I am, of course, not suggesting that West African governments throw their doors wide open to all and sundry. Especially with respect to areas of the economy dominated by migrants, it would be unrealistic to expect a government not to try and do something to reduce their domination. All I am trying to emphasize is the futility of trying to achieve this end by restriction rather than competition. For in nearly all cases where restrictive legislation has been proffered as a cure, evasion has been very common. More than this, such policies have had a most invidious effect on the nationals themselves. Few people are able to resist the temptation of earning an income just by giving their names to essentially migrant-owned enterprises, or by serving as "sleeping partners." Thus, whilst the stock of enterprise among the indigenous people is not necessarily increased by restrictive legislation, this legislation may have the more negative effect of breeding a class of "economic parasites" in the country.

Much of what I have said, it may be argued, applies with equal force to other foreign enterprises in West African countries, notably those of European and Asian business houses. Am I suggesting that governments should adopt a laissez-faire attitude to their growth without any thought for the consequences of the domination of the country's economy by such large-scale foreign enterprise? Do I believe that competition rather than restriction is the way to cope with this situation? Whilst my position on the essential point remains the same, I would like to refer back to my definition of regional mobility, especially that aspect of it which I equated with horizontal social mobility. This indicates that regional mobility is assumed as occurring among peoples at about the same stage of socio-economic development. This is an important element in the discussion: first, it underlines the element of self-discovery among the immigrants and secondly, it emphasizes that the level of achievement of the migrants is not beyond the ability of the nationals, given the proper incentives and direction. The technological and management gap between large-scale European enterprises and the relatively small-scale African businesses imposes a different dimension to the problems posed by their domination of the economy of a country.

Conclusion

The contribution to economic development of foreign, non-local enterprise, not only of the large-scale European type but also of the small-scale African type, is a subject that should receive more and more attention from scholars. In the final analysis, the only way real development can take place in Africa is by the Africans themselves improving or transforming the social and economic structure of their society. And the only way scholars can help in this venture is first to try and understand the various ways and circumstances through which the societies have in the past transformed their economy themselves, and how they will continue to do so in the present. I believe that regional mobility is a significant transforming experience not only for the individuals concerned but also for the communities from which they come and to which they go. Only a rounded social-science approach can help to fully illuminate the significance of this important aspect of the development process in West Africa.

A SELECTED BIBLIOGRAPHY

Ardener, Edwin and Shirley, and Warmington, W. A. *Plantation and Village Life in the Cameroons: Some Economic and Social Studies.* London: Oxford University Press, Nigerian Institute of Social and Economic Research, 1960.

Bohannan, Paul. "The Migration and Expansion of the Tiv." *Africa,* 24, no. 1 (January 1954): 2-16.

Browne, Granville St. John Orde. *Labour Conditions in West Africa.* Cmd. 6227. London: HMSO, Colonial Office, 1941.

Carreira, Antonio, and Meireles, Artur-Martins de. "Quelques notes sur les mouvements migratoires des populations de la province portugaise de Guinée." *Bulletin de l'Institut Français d'Afrique Noire (IFAN),* 22, Series B (July–October 1960): 379-92.

Colson, Elizabeth. "Migration in Africa: Trends and Possibilities." In *Population in Africa: Report of a Seminar Held at Boston University,* eds. Frank B. Lorimer and Mark Carp. Boston: Boston University Press, 1960.

Coppet, Marcel de. "Aspects sociaux de l'attraction excerce par les centres urbains en voie d'industrialisation de Dakar et de Thies, au Senegal et au Soudan." *International Institute of Political and Social Science Concerning Countries of Differing Civilisations,* 27 (1952): 297-303.

Cornevin, R. "A Successful Transfer of Labour: Cabrais Colonisation in the Trust Territory of French Togoland." *Bulletin of the Inter-African Labour Institute (ILI),* 3, no. 2 (March 1956): 8-15.

Davidson, R. B. "Labour Migration in Tropical Africa." *Indian Journal of Economics,* 37, no. 147, pt. 4 (April 1957): 365-77.

———. *Migrant Labour in the Gold Coast.* Achimota, Ghana: University of Ghana, Department of Economics, 1954.

Diop, Abdoulaye. "Enquête sur la migration Toucouleur à Dakar." *Bulletin de l'IFAN,* 22, Series B (July–October 1960): 393-418.

Elkan, Walter. Migrant Labour in Africa: An Economist's Approach." *Papers and Proceedings of the American Economic Association,* 49 (May 1959): 188-97.

———. "Migrant Labour South of the Sahara: The Persistence of

Migrant Labour." *Bulletin of the ILI*, 6, no. 5 (September 1959): 36-43.

——. *Migrants and Proletarians: Urban Labour in the Economic Development of Uganda*. London: Oxford University Press, East African Institute of Social Research, 1960.

Fortes, M. "Cultural Contact as a Dynamic Process: An Investigation in the Northern Territories of the Gold Coast." *Africa*, 9, no. 1 (January 1936): 24-55.

Gavrilov, N. "O migracii raboçy sily Vzapadnoj Afrike" [The Migration of Labour Forces in West Africa]. *Problemy Vostokovedenija* [Problems of Eastern Studies], 3 (1959): 82-90.

Gonzalez, Nancie L. Solien de. "Family Organization in Five Types of Migratory Wage Labor." *American Anthropologist*, 63, no. 6 (December 1961): 1264-80.

Guernier, Eugène. "L'evolution politique de l'Afrique et les mouvements de population." *International Institute of Political and Social Science Concerning Countries of Differing Civilisations*, 27 (1952): 458-65.

Harris, P. G. "The Kebbi Fishermen (Sokoto Province, Nigeria)." *Journal of the Royal Anthropological Institute*, 72, pts. 1 and 2 (1942): 23-32.

Hill, Polly. *The Gold Coast Farmer: A Preliminary Survey*. London: Oxford University Press, 1956.

——. "The Migrant Cocoa Farmers of Southern Ghana." *Africa*, 31, no. 3 (July 1961): 209-30.

——. "The Migration of Southern Ghanaian Cocoa Farmers." *Bulletin de l'IFAN*, 22, Series B (July–October 1960): 419-25.

Jarrett, H. Reginald. "The Strange Farmers of the Gambia." *Geographical Review*, 39, no. 4 (October 1949): 649-57.

Kirk-Green, A. H. M. "Tax and Travel among the Hill-Tribes of Northern Adamawa." *Africa*, 26, no. 4 (October 1956): 369-79.

Kuper, Hilda, ed. *Urbanization and Migration in West Africa*. Berkeley: University of California Press, 1965.

Lebeuf, J. P. "Recent Research on Migration in West Africa." *Migration News*, 7, no. 5 (September–October 1958): 13-17.

Le Moal, G. "Un aspect de l'immigration: La fixation de Voltaiques au Ghana." *Bulletin de l'IFAN*, 22, Series B (July-October 1960): 446-54.

Manshard, W. "Land Use Patterns and Agricultural Migration in Central Ghana (Western Gonja)." *Tijdscrift voor Economische en Sociale Geografie*, 52, no. 9 (September 1961): 225-30.

Mason, P. "Inter-Territorial Migrations of Africans South of the Sahara." *International Labour Review*, 76, no. 3 (September 1957): 292-310.

Mitchell, J. Clyde. "Migrant Labour South of the Sahara: The Causes of Labour Migration." *Bulletin of the ILI*, 6, no. 1 (January 1959): 12-46.

Morgan, W. B., and Pugh, J. C. *West Africa*. London: Methuen, 1969.

Palmer, J. H. *Notes on Strange Farmers*. Gambia Sessional Papers, no. 15 (1946). Bathurst, Gambia: Government Printer, 1946.

Panofsky, Hans E. "Migrant Labour South of the Sahara: The Significance of Labour Migration for the Economic Welfare of Ghana and the Voltaic Republic." *Bulletin of the ILI*, 7, no. 4 (July 1960): 30-45.

Pauvert, J.-Cl. "Migration et education." *Bulletin de l'IFAN*, 22, Series B (July–October 1960); 467-75.

Piault, M. P. "Migrant Labour in Africa: The Migration of Workers in West Africa." *Bulletin of the ILI*, 9, no. 1 (February 1961): 98-123.

Prothero, R. Mansell. *Migrant Labour from Sokoto Province, Northern Nigeria*. Kaduna, Nigeria: Government Printer, Northern Region of Nigeria, 1959.

———. "Migrant Labour in West Africa." *Journal of Local Administration Overseas*, 1, no. 3 (July 1962): 149-55.

———. "Migratory Labour from North-Western Nigeria." *Africa*, 27, no. 3 (July 1957): 251-61.

Read, Margaret. "Migrant Labour in Africa and Its Effects on Tribal Life." *International Labour Review*, 45, no. 6 (June 1942): 605-31.

Rouch, Jean. "Migrations au Ghana (Enquête 1953–55)." *Journal de la Société des Africanistes*, 26, fasc. 1 and 2 (1956): 33-196.

———. "Problèmes relatifs à l'étude des migrations traditionelles et des migrations actuelles en Afrique occidentale." *Bulletin de l'IFAN*, 22, Series B (July–October 1960): 369-78.

———. "Les Sorkawa, pêcheurs itinérants du moyen Niger" [The Sorkawa, Migrant Fishermen of the Middle Niger]. *Africa*, 20, no. 1 (January 1950): 5-25.

Savonnet, Georges. "La colonisation du pays Koulango (Haute Côte d'Ivoire) part les Lobi de Haute-Volta." *Les Cahiers d'Outre Mer*, 15, no. 57 (January-March 1962): 25-46.

Skinner, Elliott P. "Labour Migration and Its Relationship to Socio-Cultural Change in Mossi Society." *Africa*, 30, no. 4 (October 1960): 375-401.

Southall, Adrian, ed. *Social Change in Modern Africa*. London: Oxford University Press, 1961.

Stenning, Derrick J. "Transhumance, Migratory Drift, Migration: Patterns of Pastoral Fulani Nomadism." *Journal of the Royal Anthropological Institute*, 87, pt. 1 (1957): 57-74.

Thomas, L.-V. "Esquisse sur les mouvements de population et les contracts socio-culturels en pays Diola (Basse-Casamance)" [Sketch of Population Movements and Socio-Cultural Contacts in the Territory of the Diola (Lower Casamance)]. *Bulletin de l'IFAN*, 22, Series B (July–October 1960): 486-508.

Tidjani, A. Serpos. "A Glimpse of Migration between Dahomey and Nigeria." *Migration News*, 7, no. 5 (September–October 1958): 8-11.

———. "Note sur la migration humaine à la côte du Bénin." *Bulletin de l'IFAN*, 22, Series B (July–October 1960): 509-13.

Turner, H. W. "The Church of the Lord: The Expansion of a Nigerian Independent Church in Sierra Leone and Ghana." *Journal of African History*, 3, no. 1 (1962): 91-110.

Udo, R. K. "The Migrant Tenant Farmers in Eastern Nigeria." *Africa*, 34, no. 4 (October 1964): 326-39.

Ward, Barbara. "Some Notes on Migration from Togoland." *African Affairs*, 49, no. 195 (April 1950): 129-35.

Wigny, Pierre. "Migratory Movements in Underdeveloped Countries in Course of Industrialization." *International Labour Review*, 68, no. 1 (July 1953): 1-13.

INDEX

151

Date Due

Printed in P. E. I. by ISLAND OFFSET .